THE COMPLETE BOOK OF
ORIGAMI
ANIMALS

THE COMPLETE BOOK OF
ORIGAMI ANIMALS

David Woodroffe

Constable • London

Constable & Robinson Ltd
55-56 Russell Square
London WC1B 4HP

First published in the UK in 2013 by Constable,
an imprint of Constable & Robinson Ltd

A copy of the British Library Cataloguing in Publication Data is
available from the British Library

ISBN 978-1-47210-911-8

Printed and bound in the EU

10 9 8 7 6 5 4 3 2 1

Contents

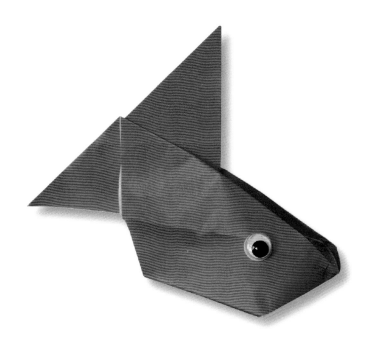

Contents

Introduction

When the Chinese first developed paper, probably around the second century BC, we can be pretty sure that they folded and wrapped things in it long before they thought to write on it! We know that they were making folded paper models from very early on as there is evidence that they burned paper replicas of things like boats and hats at funerals up until the 13th century.

Introduction

The paper making process spread to Europe at about this time, too, and we know that folded paper models were made there in the 15th century. But it was in Japan, in the 17th century, that the art of Origami really took off, where the Japanese for 'folding' is *ori* and 'paper' is *kami*. We know that they made paper butterflies for Shinto weddings, so we can assume that paper folding was an important part of Japanese ceremonies by that time. Samurai warriors would exchange gifts with noshi attached. These were small folded paper tokens that wished the recipient good luck; a custom that survives to this day in Japan when presents are given.

Three examples of modern day noshi. The one on the right is a 'wedding noshi' which depicts a tortoise and a crane, both symbols of good luck in Japan

These days most origami models are made from a square piece of paper but traditional origami models were less conventional and often started with a pre-shaped piece of paper. Sometimes glue was also used and the paper was cut further during the process of making the model. This form of paper sculpture is known as kirigami, *kiri* being Japanese for 'cut'. For our book every model is created from a paper square, although a few of the projects need a couple of cuts with a pair of scissors, for which I apologise in advance to the purists who consider any cutting to be kirigami, but I feel that the models where I've used it all benefit in appearance for doing so.

Each model instruction comes with a photograph showing the final model plus step-by-step instructions that take you through each stage of the folding process. The models are graded from very simple to quite difficult but, with practice, and by making them in sequence, your origami skills can improve, allowing you to impress everyone with your models!

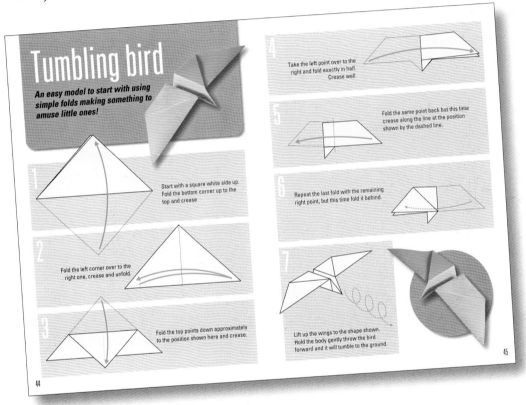

I came to origami relatively recently and sometimes struggled with poor or non-existent written instructions, and with unsatisfactory diagrams that gave me no clue as to what I should be doing. They often bore no resemblance to the strange-looking piece of paper I held in my hand but, to be fair, that was quite often due to my own bad interpretation of what I was supposed to be doing! So I have tried to go back to basics and sometimes may have over-simplified the instructions, but in doing this I hope to get you around the problems that I stumbled through when I first started.

Spend some time studying the section on 'Folds' and familiarise yourself with what the symbols and lines mean before starting out on the models.

Introduction

You will probably discover, as I have, that origami can become a little addictive as well as being a different and pleasant form of relaxation. So if you feel you want to develop your skills to a higher level you will find a wealth of information about origami on the internet and in many other excellent publications that go beyond the animals and birds that we have shown in this book.

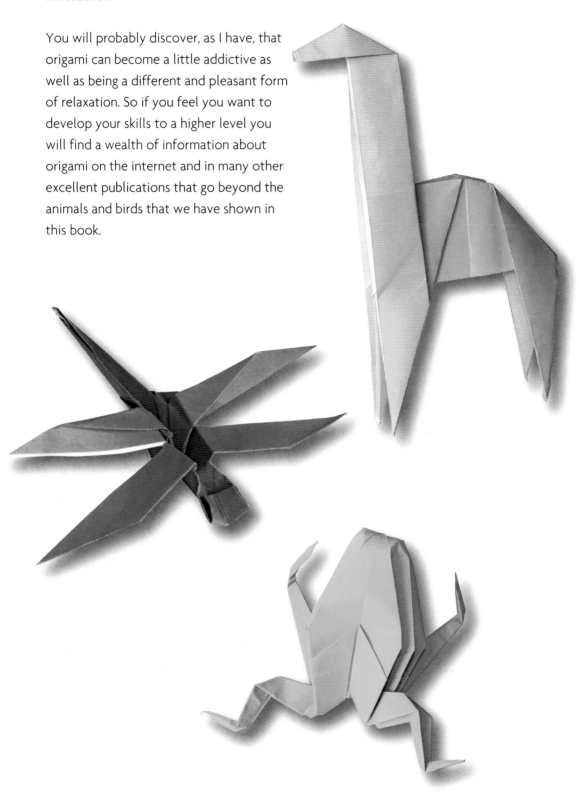

Finally, I need to thank the many origami experts past and present who, through their books and personal instruction, have introduced me to the fascinating art of paper folding. This book has been compiled almost exclusively from other sources of traditional origami which in itself has proved to be an exhaustive task. Among those who have sustained my enthusiasm I am particularly grateful to Ray Rich for his design input, to my editor Rod Green, to my daughter Laura and son Matthew for their continuing support and encouragement, and to Sonya, whose inspiration through long days of producing the diagrams saved me from folding up!

Paper

The only thing that we need to create an origami model is *kami* or 'paper'. Luckily for us, paper is cheap, easily available and comes in many different colours and patterns. The animal and bird models shown in this book were all made from special origami paper, which can be bought from specialist craft and hobby shops or purchased through the internet. This proved to be the best paper to use for the following reasons. Firstly, the paper is the perfect weight and thickness, about 70 to 80 gsm, and it folds easily and crisply. You can buy it in packs containing hundreds of sheets and in many different bright colours. It also comes in different sizes, although for this book all the models were made from what seems to be the commonest size of 150 mm (6 inches) square, which worked out to be the ideal size for creating them.

Coloured origami paper

Patterned origami paper

The tortoise and cicada made with patterned origami paper

Lastly, origami paper is usually coloured on one side and white on the other, and you will see that this can be used to great effect in models such as the cicada and the penguin.

Paper

Another type of paper which you can use is gift wrapping paper. This is inexpensive and is also the perfect weight and density. It comes in bright colours and great patterns that can be used to make some models far more attractive. The only problem with wrapping paper is that you will have to cut it down to size, but I demonstrate a way of doing this later in the book.

Butterflies made from gift wrapping paper

Copier paper is another alternative. This normally comes in white, but it is possible to buy it in colour packs. As well as being generally heavier than origami paper it has a softer quality that doesn't make such crisp folds, but this may just be a personal observation. Also you will need to cut accurate squares from the A4 sheets. Again, I show this later in the book.

The lizard head made from white copier paper

A mouse made from newspaper

Old telephone directories and newspapers are a good supply of paper to practice on, rather than using your best origami paper. These also will have to be accurately cut into perfect squares.

A swan made from a page of a telephone directory

A fish and seahorse made from foil paper

You can buy shiny origami paper, known as foil paper, which is a thin sheet of metallic foil bonded to a sheet of thin white paper. This has the ability, due to the metallic foil, to keep its shape better when folded, whereas the folds in ordinary paper will slowly creep open over time. The downside to foil paper is that it can sometimes give the models an unnatural appearance because of the reflections that its shiny surface produces. Some modellers use it all the time, especially for models of things like insects where the glossy finish can make them much more realistic.

Most light papers are suitable for origami, but some textured paper won't hold a fold too well. So experiment with anything you happen to lay your hands on. You may discover something that's perfect for the look you want a particular model to have.

Tools

Not much to talk about here! Basically you will need a pair of hands and maybe something to make sharp folds. I crease my folds with the flat of my thumb nail, but some people like to use folding bones. These are small wooden or plastic spatulas used to crease the paper. If you're doing lots of models in one go then one of these could be a great help. They come in many shapes and sizes and it comes down to personal taste which one to use.

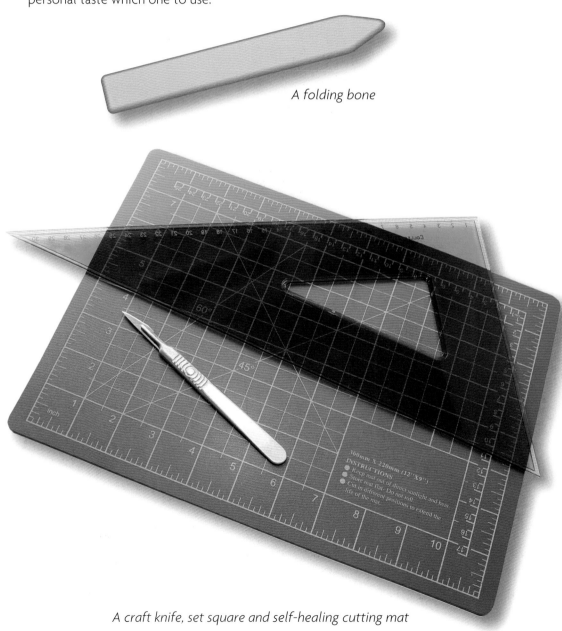

A folding bone

A craft knife, set square and self-healing cutting mat

If you are going to be cutting out squares from wrapping paper or newspaper then you will need a sharp craft knife, a good set square, preferably with a scale, and a flat surface that you can cut on. Self-healing cutting mats are perfect for this and an A4 one is the perfect size and is not expensive.

A good pair of scissors will be essential for cutting the models when needed.

Stick on eyes, otherwise known as 'wobbly' or 'googly' eyes, can make some models look cuter and more fun. They can be bought in different sizes for a relatively low cost. Some are self-adhesive while others will need glue to attach them to the model. Other-wise you can just draw eyes on with a felt tip pen.

Folds

What the lines and symbols mean, and how to fold them.

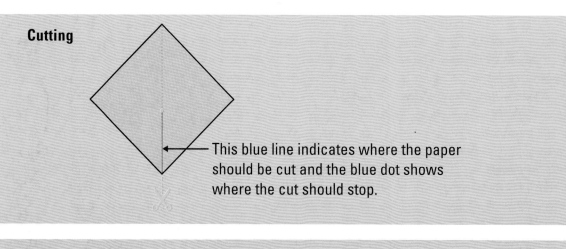

Cutting

This blue line indicates where the paper should be cut and the blue dot shows where the cut should stop.

These are the two types of fold you will need to know

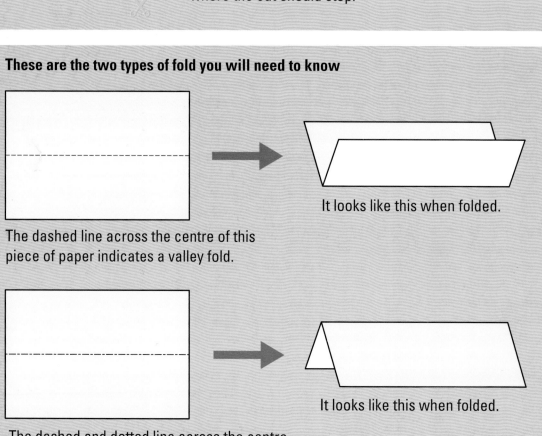

It looks like this when folded.

The dashed line across the centre of this piece of paper indicates a valley fold.

It looks like this when folded.

.The dashed and dotted line across the centre of this piece of paper indicates a mountain fold.

This diagram shows how they appear on the model instructions

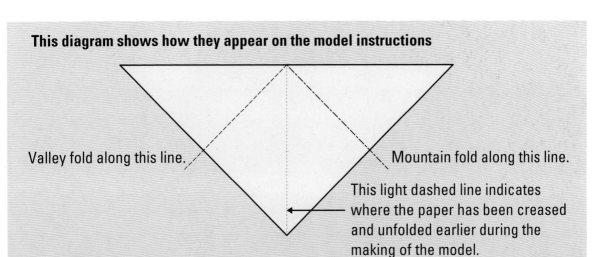

Valley fold along this line.

Mountain fold along this line.

This light dashed line indicates where the paper has been creased and unfolded earlier during the making of the model.

This diagram shows how they fold and what the arrows mean

This dotted line indicates where the flap was before being folded over.

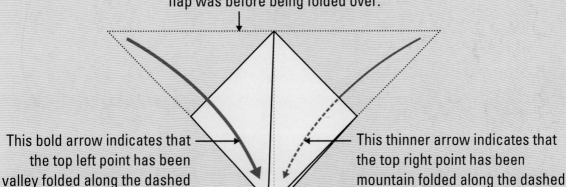

This bold arrow indicates that the top left point has been valley folded along the dashed line, forward and over to the bottom corner.

This thinner arrow indicates that the top right point has been mountain folded along the dashed and dotted line, backward and behind to the bottom corner.

This heavy arrow shows that the top left point has been valley folded over to the top right point, creased and then unfolded.

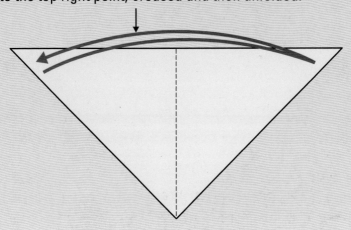

Turning the model over

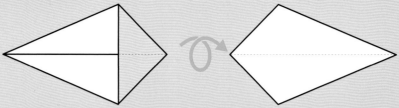

This symbol indicates that the model turns over from left to right.

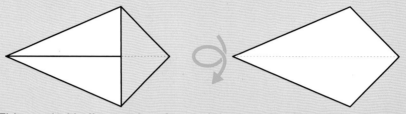

This symbol indicates that the model turns over from top to bottom.

Making an 'inside reverse' fold

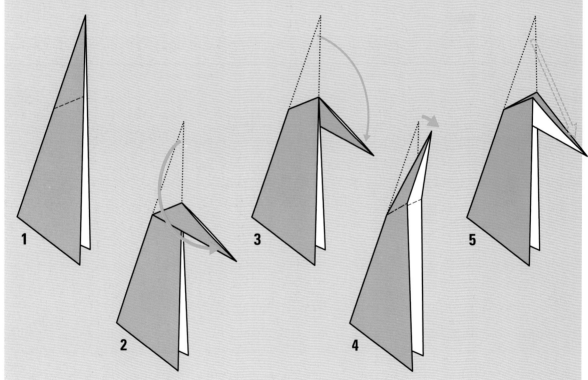

1 The dashed line indicates where the fold should be made.
2 Fold the flap forwards, crease and unfold.
3 Fold the flap backwards, crease and unfold.
4 Open the part and push the top point down.
5 Push it down until it is inside itself and crease.

Making an 'outside reverse' fold

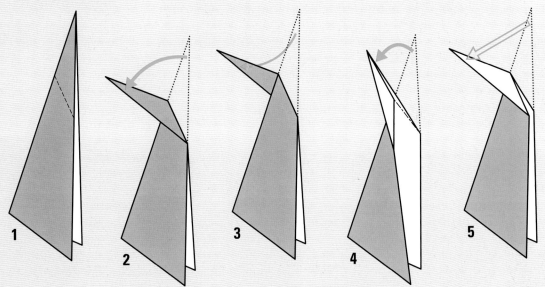

1   The dashed line indicates where the fold should be made.
2   Fold the flap forwards, crease and unfold.
3   Fold the flap backwards, crease and unfold.
4   Open the part and push the top point back.
5   Push it down until it is outside itself and crease.

Making a 'crimp' fold as used on the Seahorse

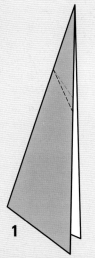 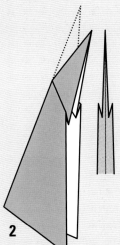 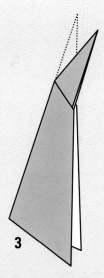

1   The dashed lines indicate where the folds should be made. Fold, crease and unfold, forwards and backwards, as in the previous folds. Do this along both dashed lines.
2   Open the part and push the top point down so that the top creases (shown in red in **1**) go inside the lower ones as shown.
3   Flatten and crease.

Cutting out a perfect square

From a sheet of A4 paper.

1

Fold the top edge down and across to the right edge. Align them accurately and then carefully crease.

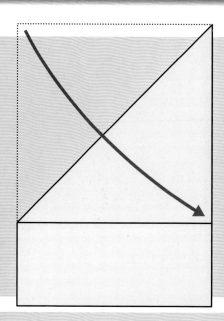

2

Unfold.

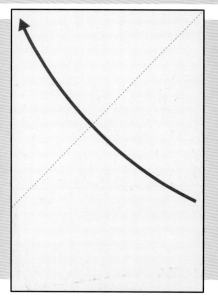

3

Now bring the top edge down to align with the left edge and crease.

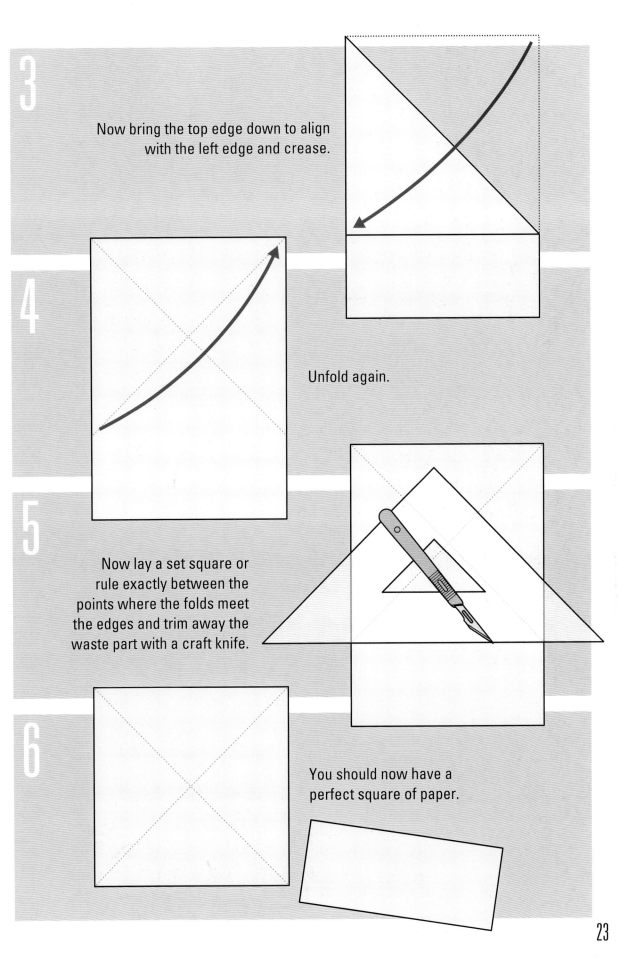

4

Unfold again.

5

Now lay a set square or rule exactly between the points where the folds meet the edges and trim away the waste part with a craft knife.

6

You should now have a perfect square of paper.

Cutting out a perfect square

From gift wrapping paper or newspaper.

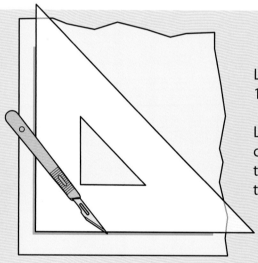

Let's imagine you want to cut a 150 mm (6 inch) square.

Lay the set square on the paper and cut the paper along the two sides that are at right angles, cutting further than the 150 mm (6 inches) required.

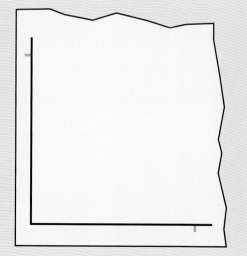

Now measure and accurately mark off 150 mm (6 inches) along each side from the corner.

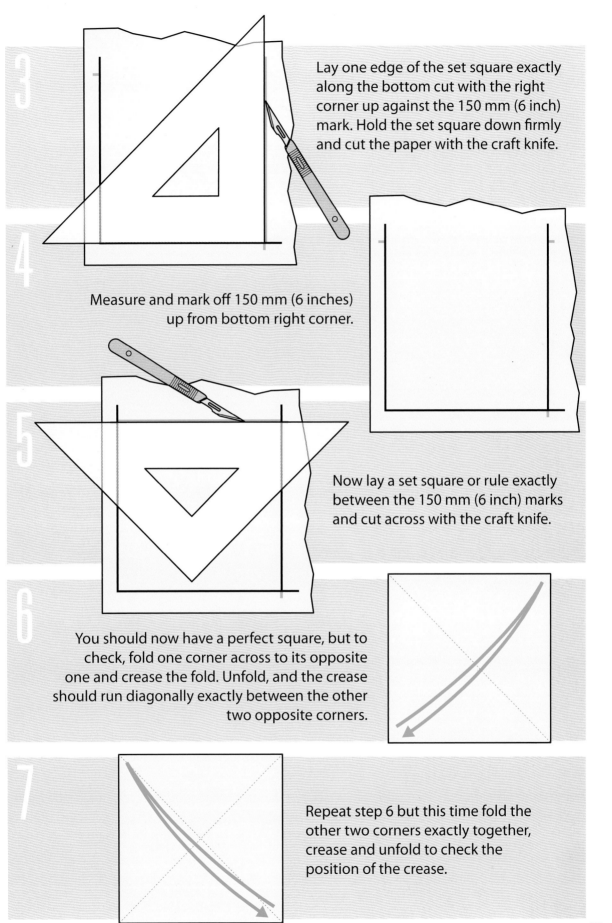

3 Lay one edge of the set square exactly along the bottom cut with the right corner up against the 150 mm (6 inch) mark. Hold the set square down firmly and cut the paper with the craft knife.

4 Measure and mark off 150 mm (6 inches) up from bottom right corner.

5 Now lay a set square or rule exactly between the 150 mm (6 inch) marks and cut across with the craft knife.

6 You should now have a perfect square, but to check, fold one corner across to its opposite one and crease the fold. Unfold, and the crease should run diagonally exactly between the other two opposite corners.

7 Repeat step 6 but this time fold the other two corners exactly together, crease and unfold to check the position of the crease.

Fold me...

Model instructions

Tumbling bird

An easy model to start with using simple folds to make something that will amuse smaller children!

1 Start with a square white side up. Fold the bottom corner up to the top and crease

2 Fold the left corner over to the right one, crease and unfold.

3 Fold the top points down approximately to the position shown here and crease.

4

Take the left point over to the right and fold exactly in half. Crease well.

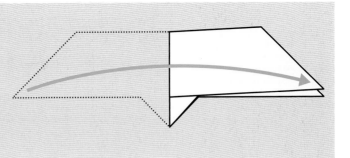

5

Fold the same point back but this time crease along the line at the position shown by the dashed line.

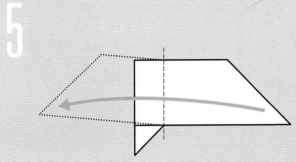

6

Repeat the last fold with the remaining right point, but this time folding it behind.

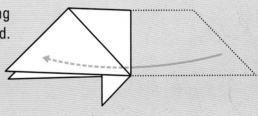

7

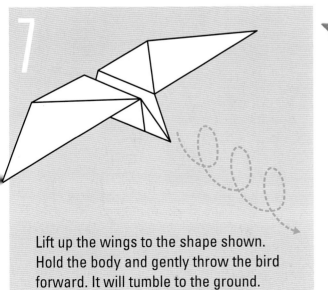

Lift up the wings to the shape shown. Hold the body and gently throw the bird forward. It will tumble to the ground.

Cicada

This model of the tree cricket that's found in warmer climates uses the same first two folds as the tumbling bird.

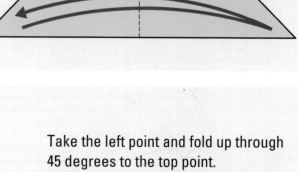

1

Start with a square white side up. Fold the bottom corner up to the top and crease.

2

Fold the left point over to the right one, crease and unfold.

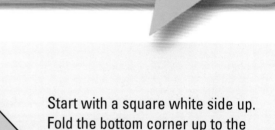

3

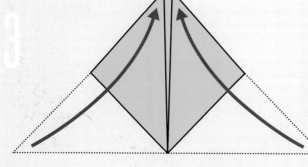

Take the left point and fold up through 45 degrees to the top point.
Repeat with the right point and crease both folds.

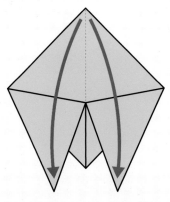

Fold down the front top points to the positions shown and crease.

Take the front top corner down as shown and crease.

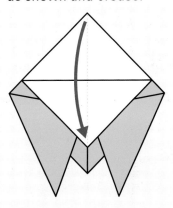

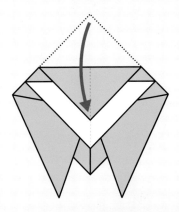

Take the remaining top corner down as shown and crease.

Turn the model over and fold the two angled edges to the centre and crease well.

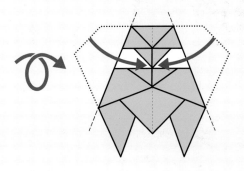

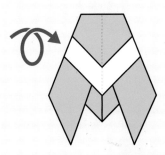

Turn the model over again and it's finished!

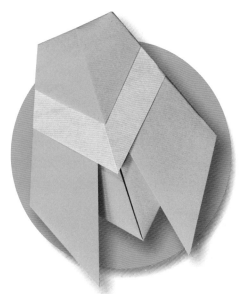

Fox

The first two folds in the model of the cicada are used again to start this cute little fox!

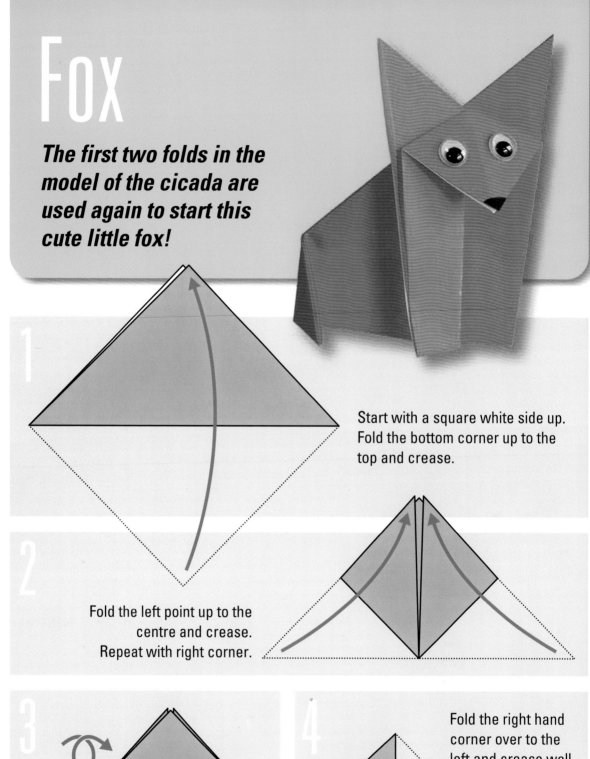

1

Start with a square white side up. Fold the bottom corner up to the top and crease.

2

Fold the left point up to the centre and crease. Repeat with right corner.

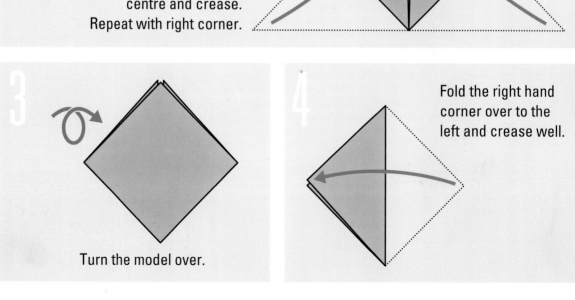

3

Turn the model over.

4

Fold the right hand corner over to the left and crease well.

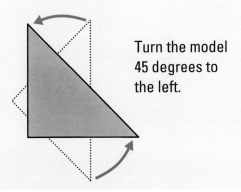

Turn the model 45 degrees to the left.

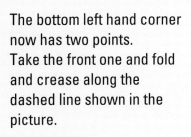

The bottom left hand corner now has two points. Take the front one and fold and crease along the dashed line shown in the picture.

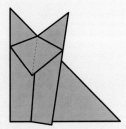

As you do this the top middle point will be forced downwards.

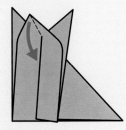

When the fold in instruction 6 has been creased you flatten and crease the middle point to make the head.

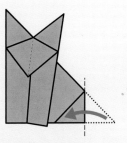

Fold and crease the right hand point to make tail.

Add a nose and some eyes to complete the model.

Duck

A simple, but realistic model!

1

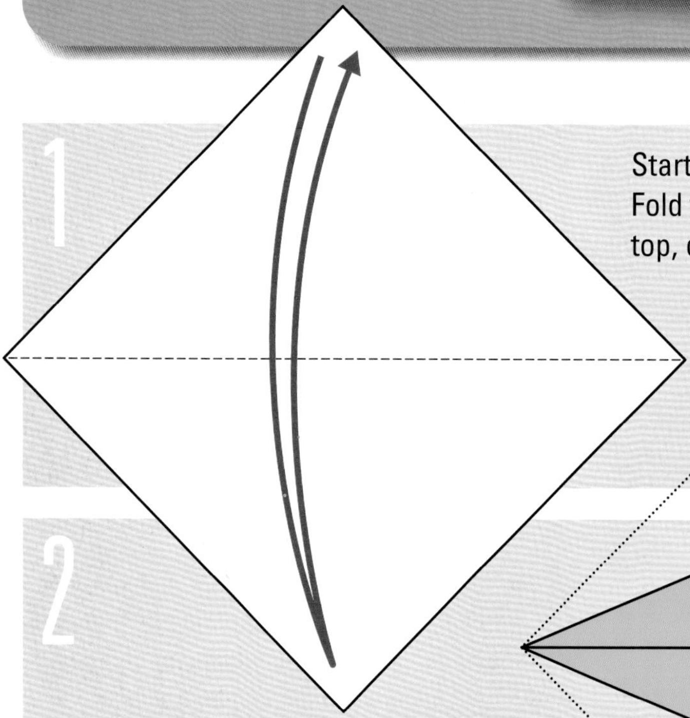

Start with a square white side up. Fold the bottom corner up to the top, crease and unfold.

2

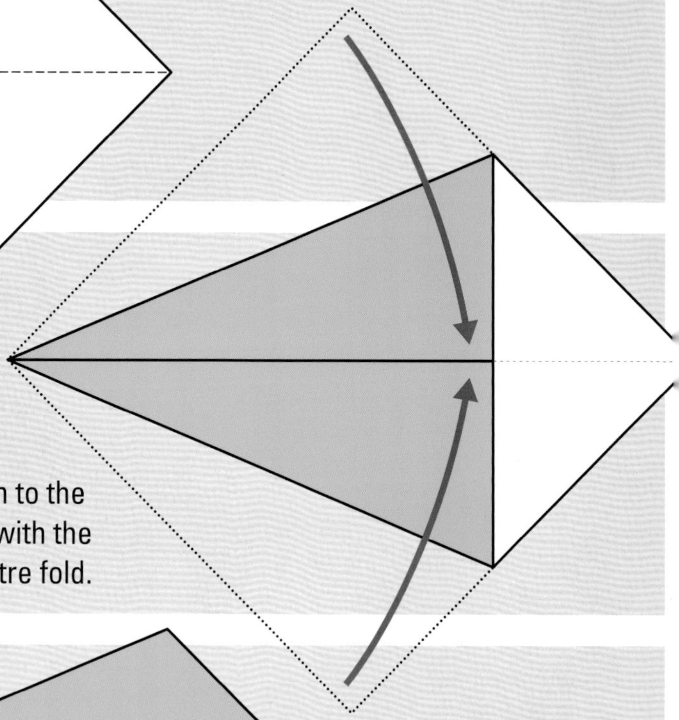

Bring the top left hand edge down to the centre fold and crease. Repeat with the bottom left edge up to the centre fold.

3

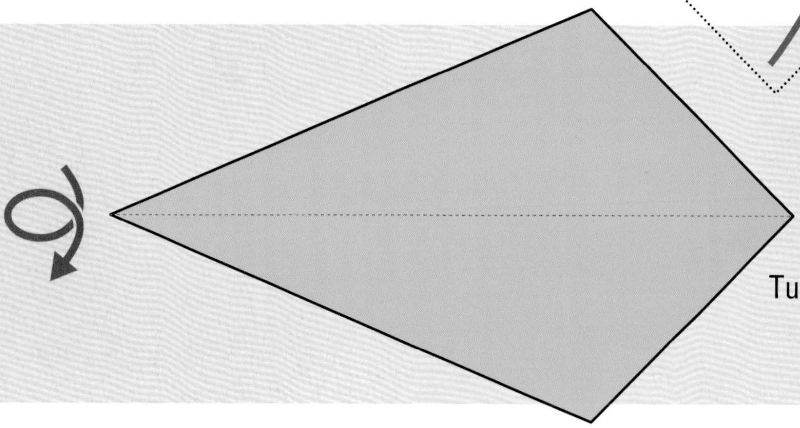

Turn the model over.

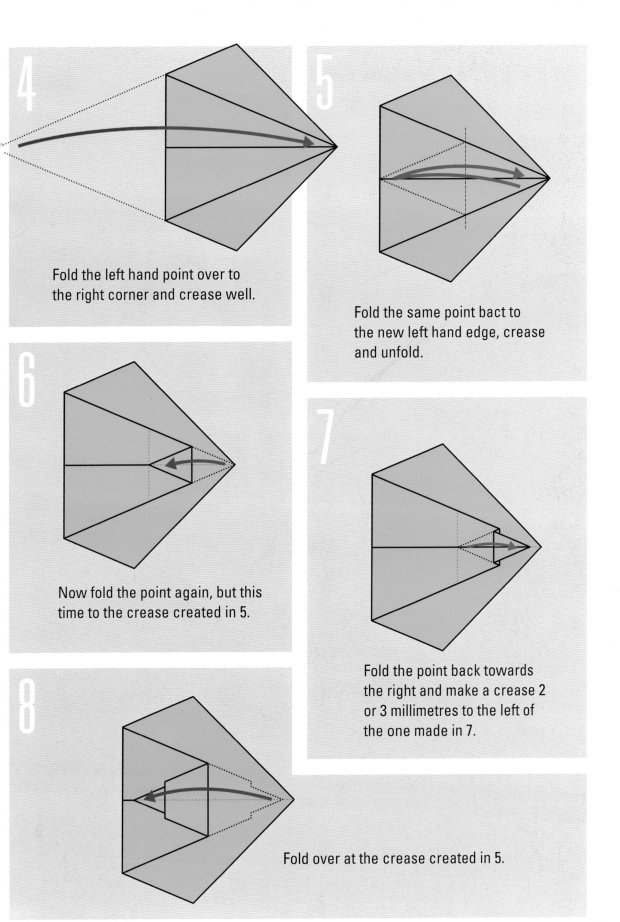

4 Fold the left hand point over to the right corner and crease well.

5 Fold the same point bact to the new left hand edge, crease and unfold.

6 Now fold the point again, but this time to the crease created in 5.

7 Fold the point back towards the right and make a crease 2 or 3 millimetres to the left of the one made in 7.

8 Fold over at the crease created in 5.

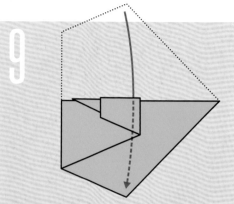

9

Fold everything in half by taking the top half behind and crease well.

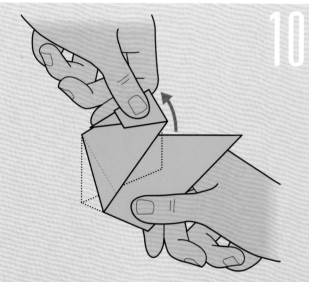

10

Grip the bottom of the model as shown with your right hand. Then with your left hand pull the beak, head and neck upwards to the position shown. Flatten a new crease at the front.

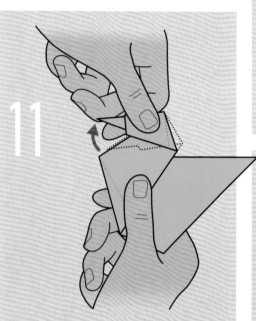

11

Grip the model with your right hand in the new position shown and with the other pull up the neck and head as shown. Flatten a new crease along the back of the head.

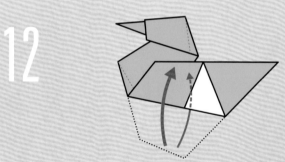

12

Fold up the front bottom edge to a level with the back and tail. Repeat with the other side.

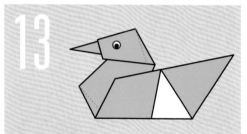

13

Maybe add eyes and your duck is complete.

Pig

This pig is a traditional origami model.

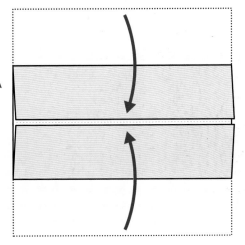

Start with a square coloured side up. Fold the bottom edge up to the top, crease and unfold.

Turn the square over and fold down the top edge to the horizontal crease in the middle. Fold up the bottom edge to the same central crease.

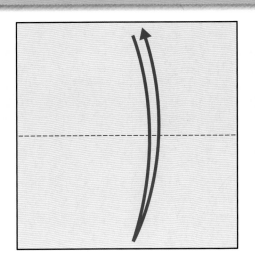

Turn the model over and then fold in the four corners as shown.

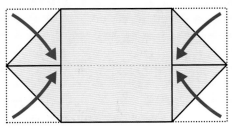

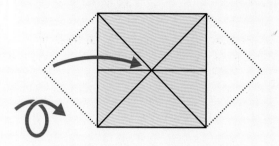

Turn the model over again and fold the left and right points into the centre and crease.

Undo the folds made in 3 and 4.

Take the left point on the top fold, shown in 5. Fold it into the centre as shown and crease flat.

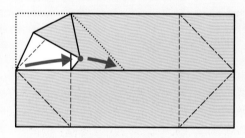

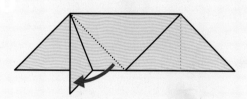

Repeat step 6 with the other 3 points.

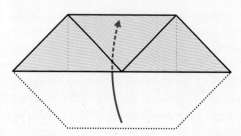

Fold the model in half by taking the bottom edge back up behind the model.

Fold down the left centre flap so that the long edge lies along the vertical crease. Crease well.

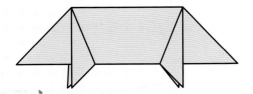

Repeat with the other three flaps to create the legs.

Crease and unfold along the dashed lines incated. Then crease the other way along the same lines and unfold.

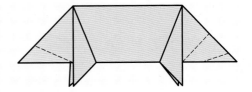

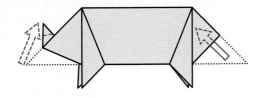

Make reverse folds along the longer lines (see 'Folds' on page 18).

Now make reverse folds along the shorter lines to complete the model.

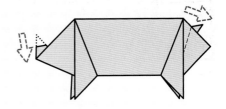

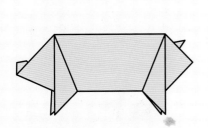

The final model should look like this.

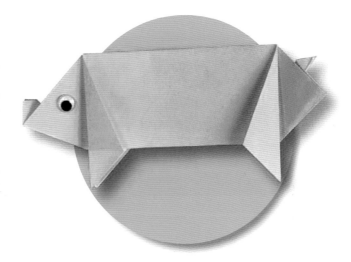

Chicken

An easy model to make but take care with steps 6 and 7.

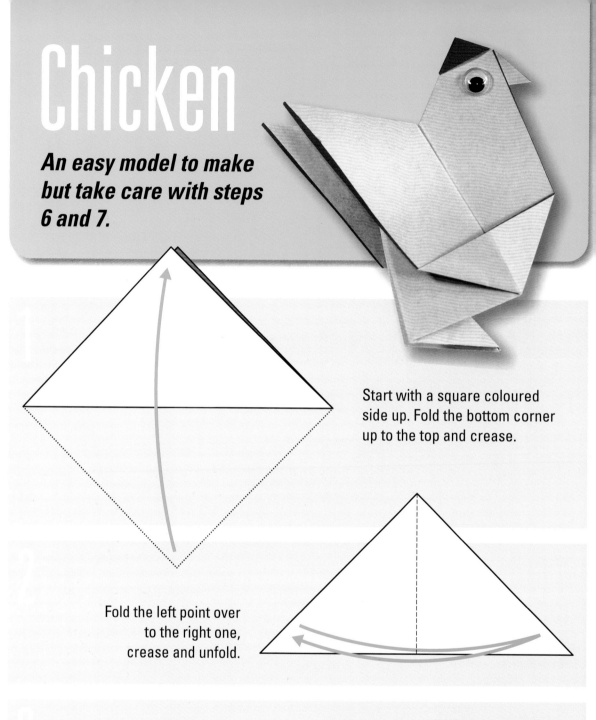

Start with a square coloured side up. Fold the bottom corner up to the top and crease.

Fold the left point over to the right one, crease and unfold.

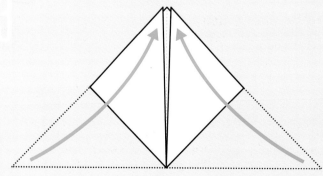

Take the left point and fold up through 45 degrees to the top point. Repeat with the right point and crease both folds.

Fold everything in half by taking the right half behind and creasing well.

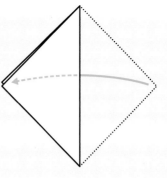

Fold, crease and unfold along the dashed line shown. Repeat, but this time fold it back, crease and unfold.

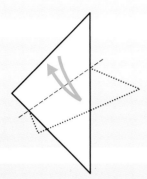

The top point now has three parts. Take the front one and fold along the crease created in 5.

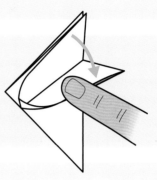

As you do action 6 the front left point will lift and curve. Flatten and crease this as shown.

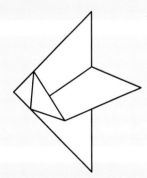

Turn the model over and repeat actions 6 and 7 on the other side.

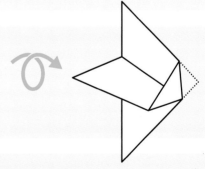

Fold, crease and unfold as shown.

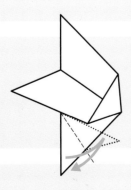

Reverse fold on the fold made in 9 and crease well.

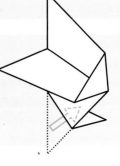

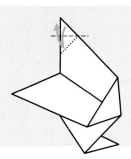

11 Fold, crease and unfold the top point.

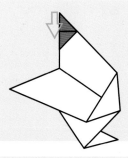

12 Carefully open the right side of the model and fold down only the outside corner.

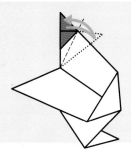

13 Fold, crease and unfold along the dashed line as indicated.

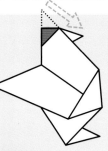

14 Open the right side of the model again and reverse fold the top point along the crease created in 13.

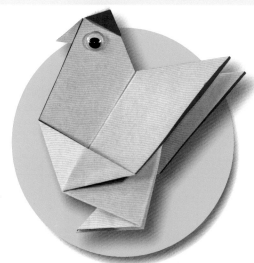

15 Draw or stick on eyes and your chicken is complete.

Seal

This model introduces a basic fold sequence (steps 1 to 6) that will be used in some later models.

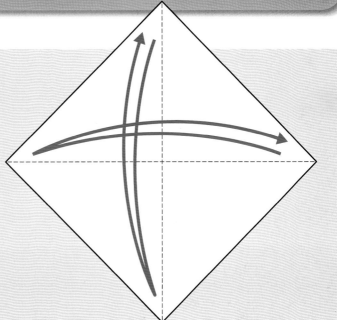

1

Start with a square, white side up, and fold the top corner down to the bottom, crease and unfold. Fold the right corner over to the left one, crease and unfold.

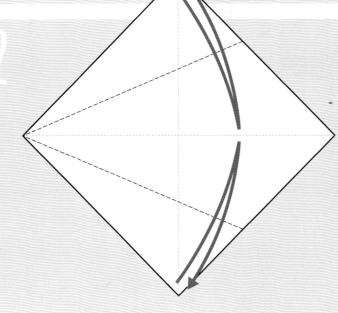

2

Bring the top left hand edge down to the centre fold, crease and unfold. Repeat with the bottom left edge up to the centre and then unfold.

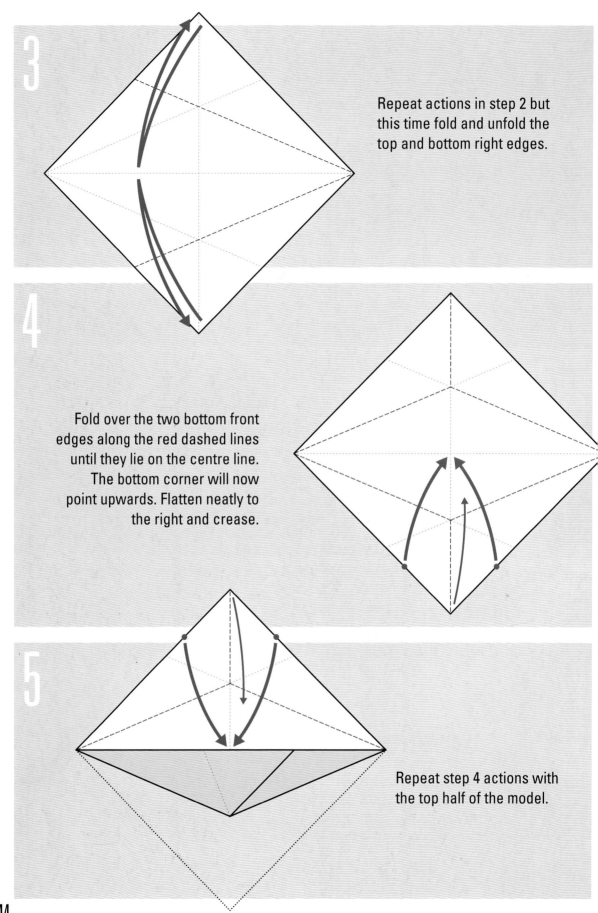

3

Repeat actions in step 2 but this time fold and unfold the top and bottom right edges.

4

Fold over the two bottom front edges along the red dashed lines until they lie on the centre line. The bottom corner will now point upwards. Flatten neatly to the right and crease.

5

Repeat step 4 actions with the top half of the model.

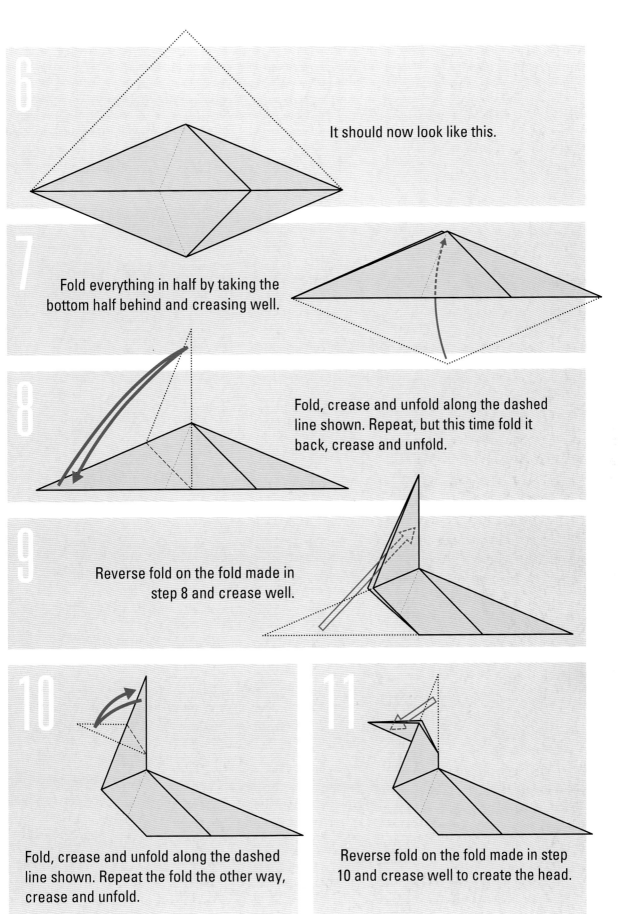

6

It should now look like this.

7

Fold everything in half by taking the bottom half behind and creasing well.

8

Fold, crease and unfold along the dashed line shown. Repeat, but this time fold it back, crease and unfold.

9

Reverse fold on the fold made in step 8 and crease well.

10

Fold, crease and unfold along the dashed line shown. Repeat the fold the other way, crease and unfold.

11

Reverse fold on the fold made in step 10 and crease well to create the head.

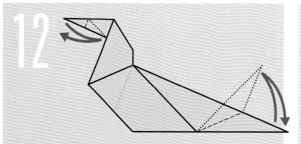

Fold, crease and unfold along the two dashed lines shown. Repeat the folds the other way, crease and unfold.

Reverse fold both the folds made in step 12 and crease well to create the nose and tail.

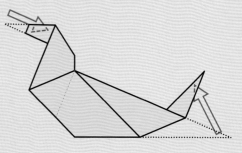

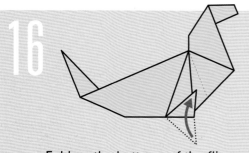

Fold down and crease the tab to create the front left flipper.

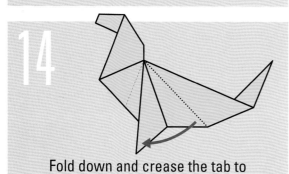

Fold up the bottoms of the flippers, crease and position at right angles.

Turn over and fold down the opposite tab.

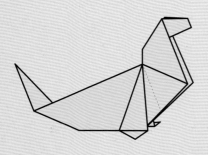

Hopefully, your seal should look something like this!

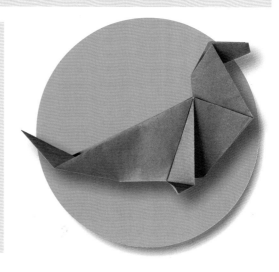

Tortoise

Another easy, but effective model that requires the use of a pair of scissors.

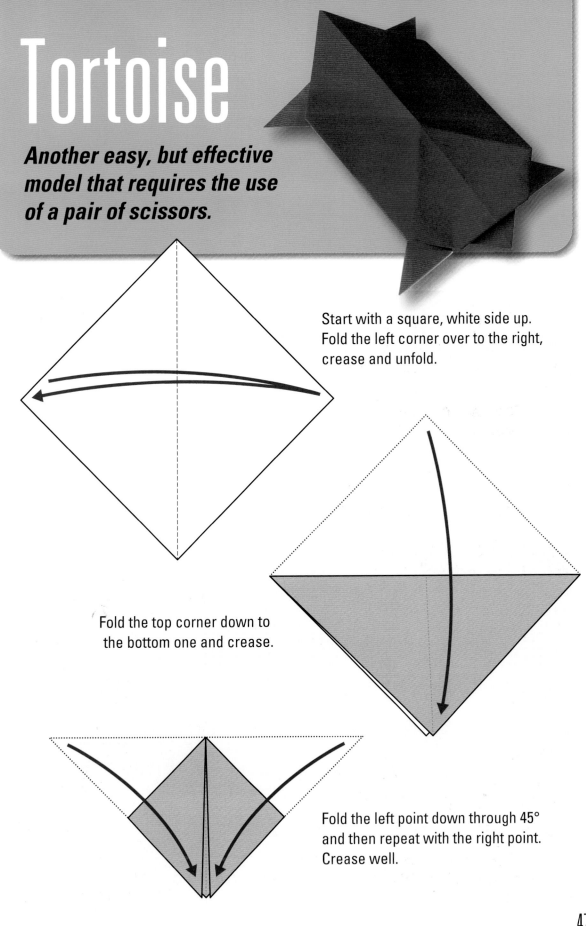

Start with a square, white side up. Fold the left corner over to the right, crease and unfold.

Fold the top corner down to the bottom one and crease.

Fold the left point down through 45° and then repeat with the right point. Crease well.

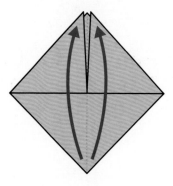

Fold the two front points at the bottom up to the top corner. Crease well.

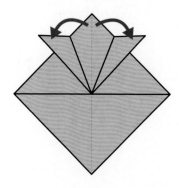

Fold the two front points, now at top, outwards as shown.

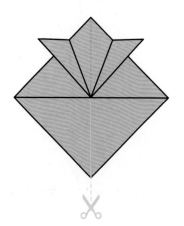

The bottom corner now has two layers. With your scissors cut along the crease on the top layer up to the up to the middle of the model.

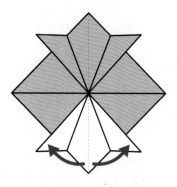

Fold the two front points at the bottom outwards as shown.

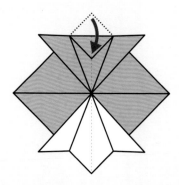

Fold down the top point along a line level with the two top flaps created in step 5.

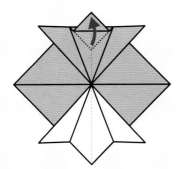

Fold up the same point along a line a couple of millimetres below the crease made in step 8.

Fold in the left and right points to the centre and crease well.

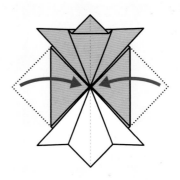

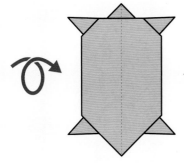

Turn over to reveal the finished tortoise.

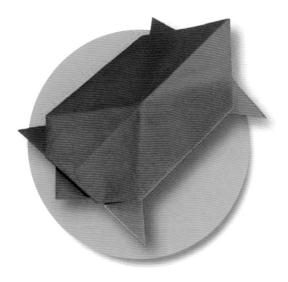

49

Penguin

By using a smaller piece of paper you can make a penguin chick.

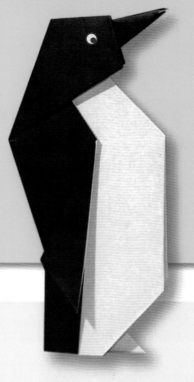

1

Start with a square coloured side up. Fold the bottom corner up to the top and crease.

2

Fold the top right hand edge down about half way and fold and crease.

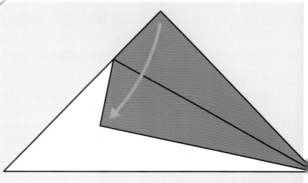

3

Take the corner you have just folded down and fold it up and crease as shown.

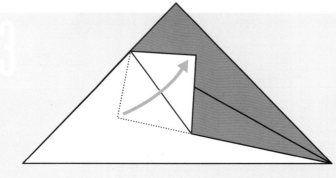

4 Turn the model over and repeat steps 2 and 3 on the other side.

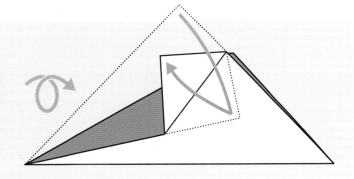

5

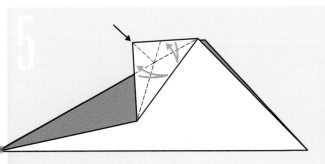

Fold the left edge of the flap created in step 5 over to the fold, crease and unfold. Repeat with the top edge down to the same fold, crease and unfold. Now crease along a line from the point to where the two previous folds cross (see arrow).

6 This step is the same as step 4 in the model of the seal. Fold over the two front edges along the folds shown in red until they lie on the centre line. The point will now point upwards. Flatten neatly towards the top and crease.

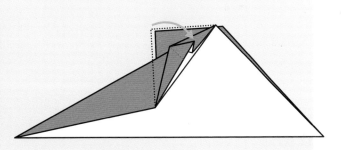

7

Turn the model over and repeat steps 6 and 7 on the other side.

8 Fold, crease and unfold as shown. Fold the other way along the same crease and then unfold.

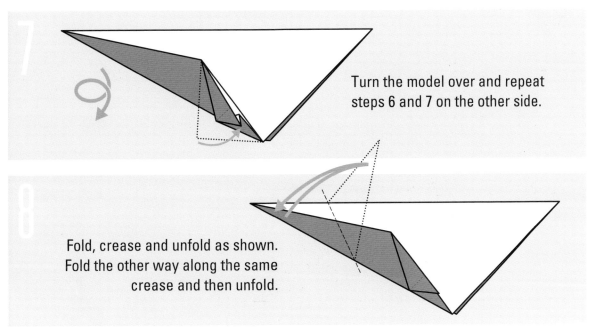

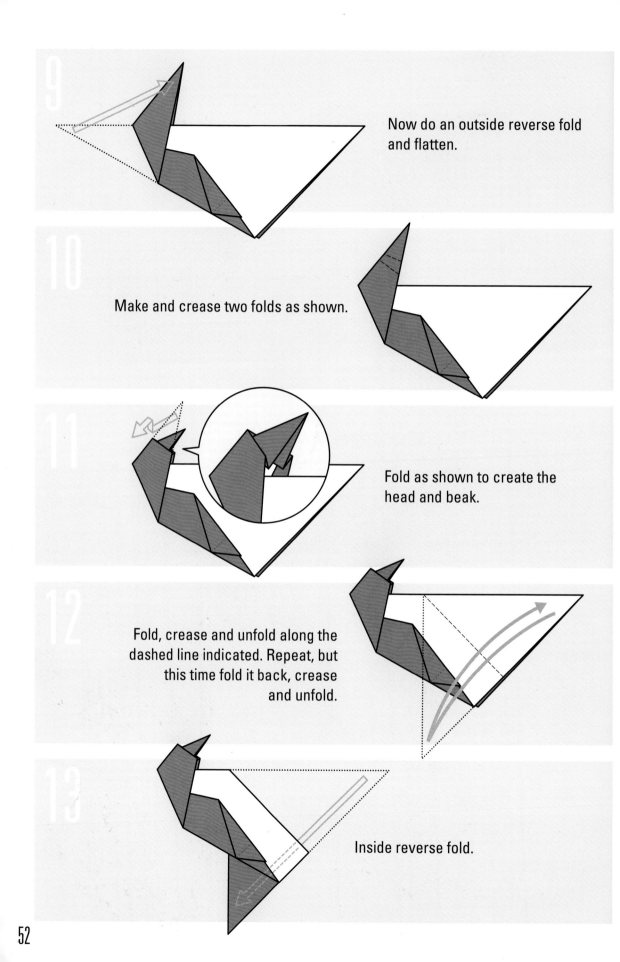

9

Now do an outside reverse fold and flatten.

10

Make and crease two folds as shown.

11

Fold as shown to create the head and beak.

12

Fold, crease and unfold along the dashed line indicated. Repeat, but this time fold it back, crease and unfold.

13

Inside reverse fold.

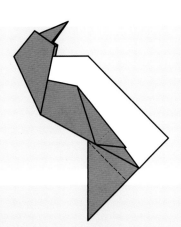

Fold, crease and unfold along the dashed line indicated. Repeat, but this time fold it back, crease and unfold.

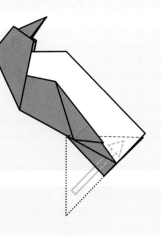

Inside reverse fold.

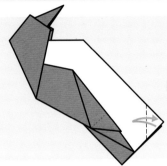

Fold, crease and unfold top point as shown.

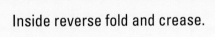

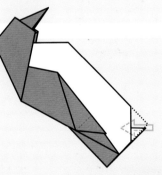

Inside reverse fold and crease.

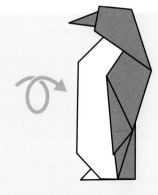

Turn the model over and repeat step 17 and the penguin is finished.

Stingray

The first fish in the book!

1

Start with a square white side up. Fold the bottom corner up to the top, crease and unfold.

2

Bring the top right hand edge down to the centre fold and crease. Repeat with the bottom right edge up to the centre fold.

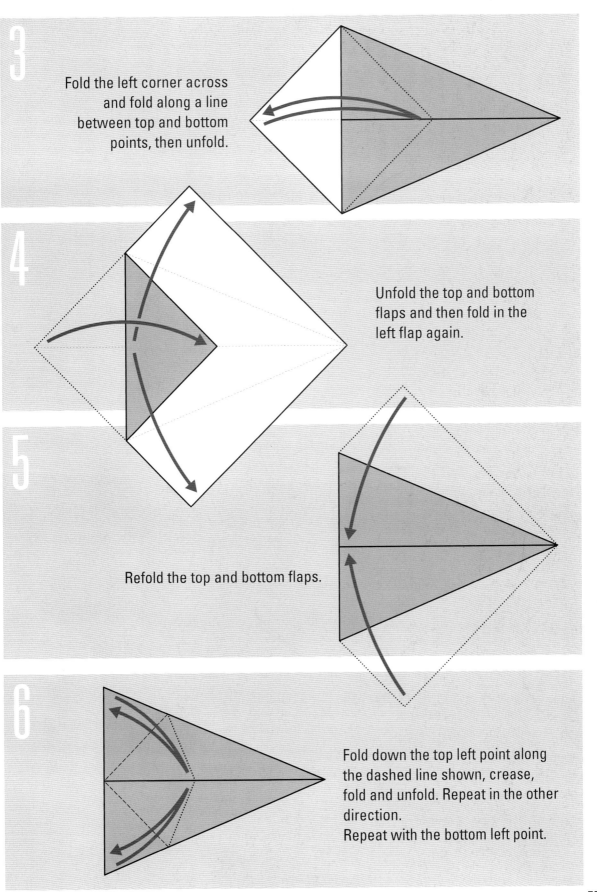

3 Fold the left corner across and fold along a line between top and bottom points, then unfold.

4 Unfold the top and bottom flaps and then fold in the left flap again.

5 Refold the top and bottom flaps.

6 Fold down the top left point along the dashed line shown, crease, fold and unfold. Repeat in the other direction.
Repeat with the bottom left point.

55

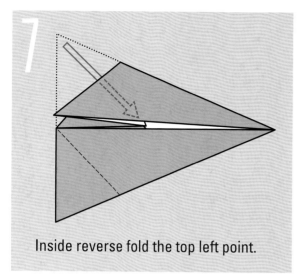

Inside reverse fold the top left point.

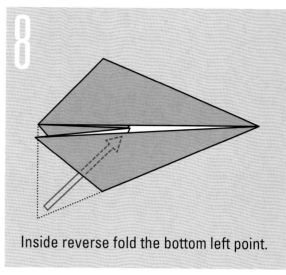

Inside reverse fold the bottom left point.

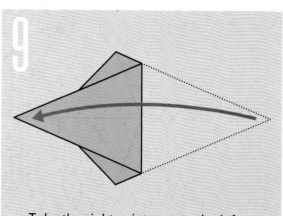

Take the right point over to the left and fold at the place shown.

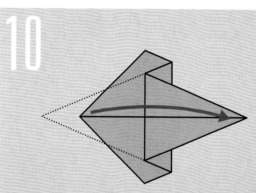

Fold the point back again along a line roughly between the top and bottom points. Crease well.

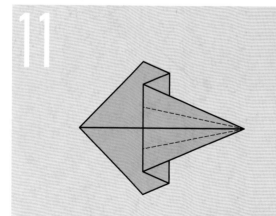

Crease and unfold each side of the tail as shown.

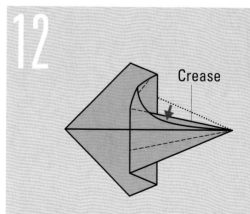

Crease

Fold the top tail over to the centre and crease it down. The end over the body will curve upwards.

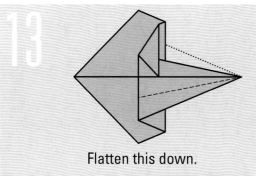

13 Flatten this down.

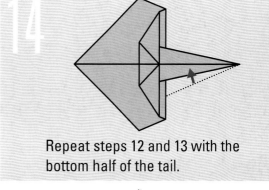

14 Repeat steps 12 and 13 with the bottom half of the tail.

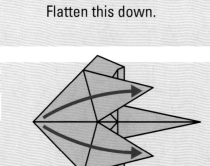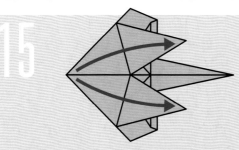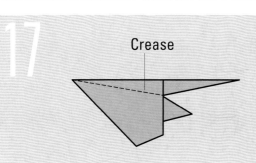

15 Fold back and crease the front two points to the position shown.

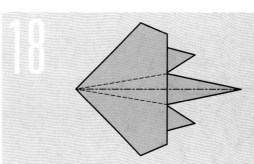

16 Fold over the top half and crease well.

Crease

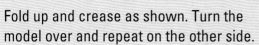

17 Fold up and crease as shown. Turn the model over and repeat on the other side.

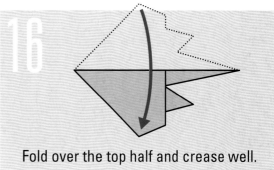

18 Shape the model like the photo and your stingray is complete.

Cow

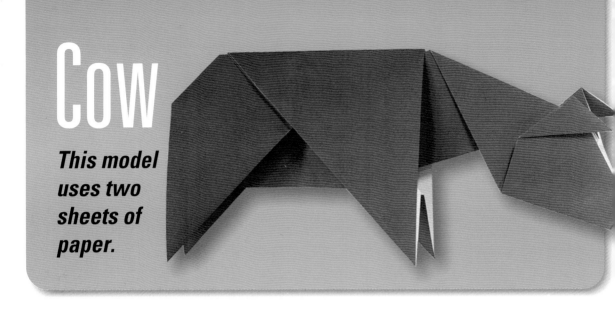

This model uses two sheets of paper.

First, the body

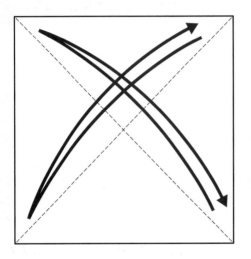

Start with a square, white side up. Fold the bottom left corner up to the top right, crease and unfold. Repeat with the bottom right corner up to the top left.

Turn the sheet over and fold the bottom edge up to the top one, crease and unfold. Repeat with the right edge over to the left one.

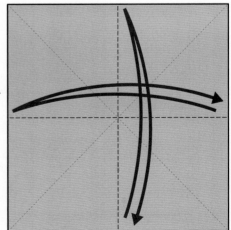

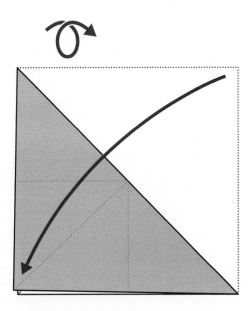

Fold the top right corner down to the bottom left one.

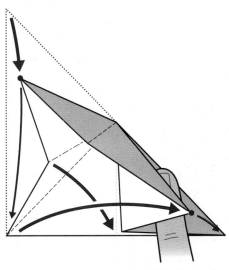

Hold the bottom right triangle and then take the top point, at bottom left, across to bottom right.
Push in the centre of the left side as shown and flatten.

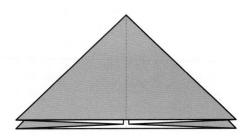

It should look like this now.

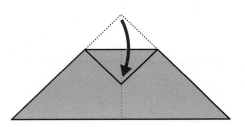

Fold down the top point about one third of the way down.
Crease well.

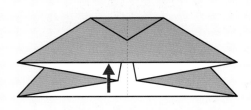

Lift up the front bottom edge.

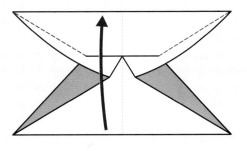

Fold it all the way open.

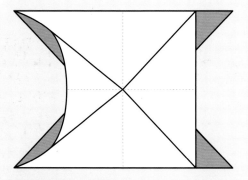

Flatten and crease the two mid points that open up.

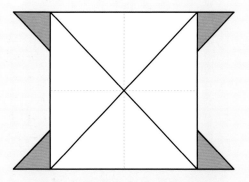

Now it should look like this.

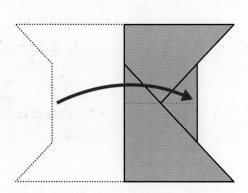

Fold in half down the middle.

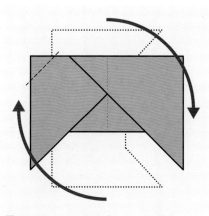

Turn the model through 90°.
Fold and crease.
Fold and crease the top left corner.
Fold and crease in the other direction and unfold.

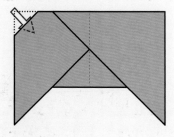

Inside reverse fold the corner.

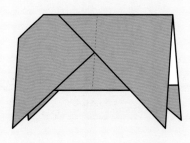

The body is now complete.

And now the head!

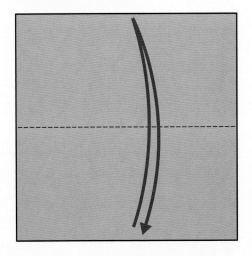

Start with a square, coloured side up. Fold the bottom edge up to the top edge, crease and unfold.

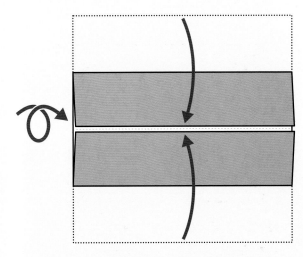

Turn the sheet over and fold the bottom edge up to the centre and crease. Repeat with the top edge down to the centre.

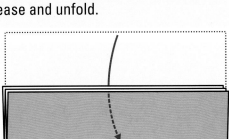

Fold the model in half by folding the top half behind.

Fold up the bottom right corner to top edge through 45° and crease.

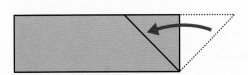

Now fold over as shown and crease. Unfold and then unfold step 4.

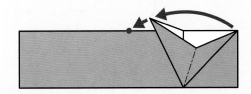

Take the front top right corner and fold across as shown, and flatten.

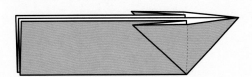

Repeat with the other side.

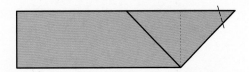

Fold and crease aong the dashed line indicated. Fold and crease in the other direction and unfold.

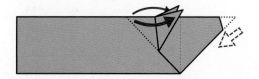

Open the underside and inside reverse fold the crease in step 8.
Fold the ears on each side.

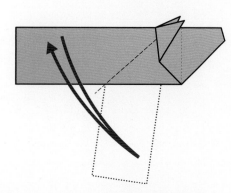

Fold and crease aong the dashed line indicated. Fold and crease in the other direction and unfold.

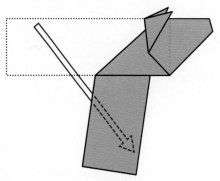

Open the underside and inside reverse fold the crease in step 10.

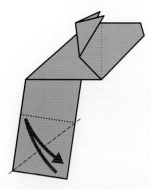

Fold and crease aong the dashed line indicated. Fold and crease in the other direction and unfold.

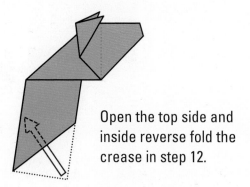

Open the top side and inside reverse fold the crease in step 12.

The head is now complete and should be joined to the body by pushing it inside the body.

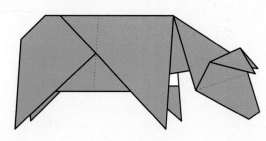

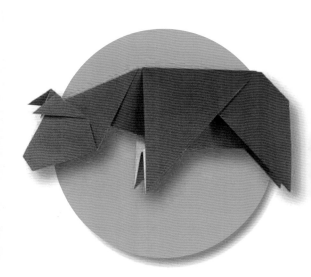

Bird

**A traditional
origami model!**

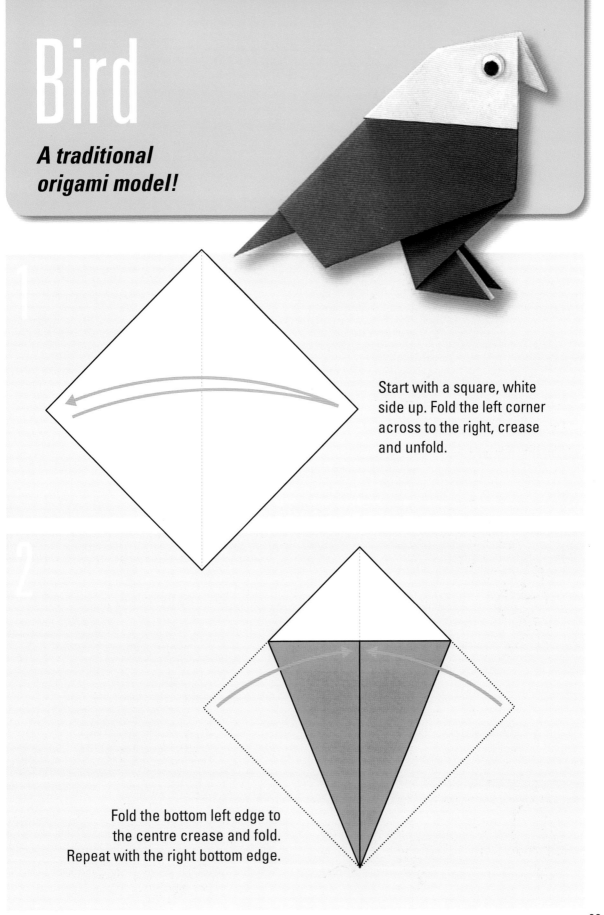

1

Start with a square, white side up. Fold the left corner across to the right, crease and unfold.

2

Fold the bottom left edge to the centre crease and fold. Repeat with the right bottom edge.

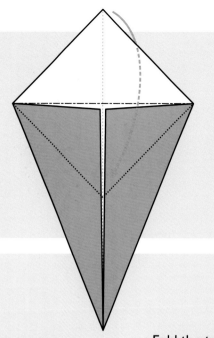

3

Now fold the top corner down behind the model and crease along a line that lies between the left and right points.

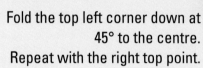

4

Fold the top left corner down at 45° to the centre. Repeat with the right top point.

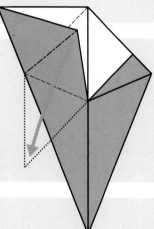

5

Unfold the left fold created in step 4. Take the front centre point, pull down and crease along a line as shown in red. Flatten.

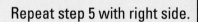

6

Repeat step 5 with right side.

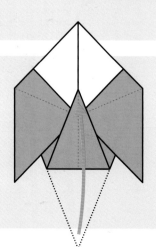

7

Fold the tip down and crease at the position shown.

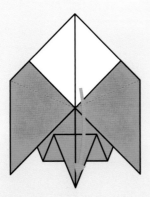

Fold the tip down and crease at the positio shown.

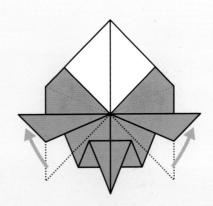

Fold up and crease the two side points.

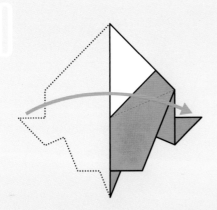

Fold the model in half by bringing the left side over the right.
Crease well.

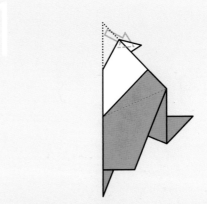

Fold and crease the top point and then inside reverse fold as shown.

Add an eye and the bird is complete.

Lizard Head

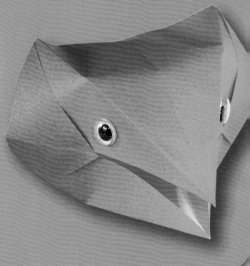

This model introduces a basic fold sequence (steps 1 to 9) that will be used in quite a few of the later models.

1

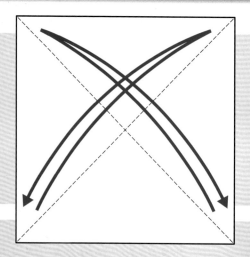

Start with a square, white side up. Fold the bottom left corner up to the top right, crease and unfold. Repeat with the bottom right corner up to the top left.

2

Fold the bottom edge up to the top one, crease and unfold. Repeat with the right edge over to the left one.

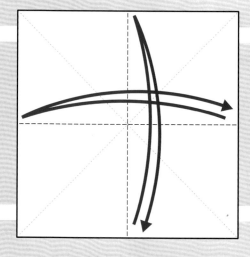

3

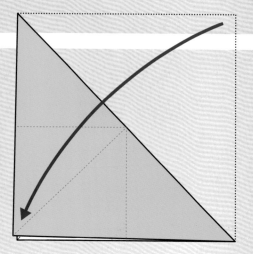

Fold the top right corner down to the bottom left one.

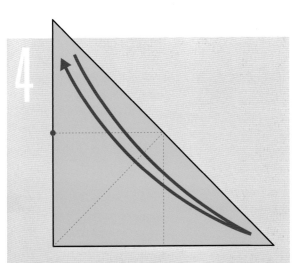

Fold the top point down at 45° to the bottom right one. Crease and unfold.

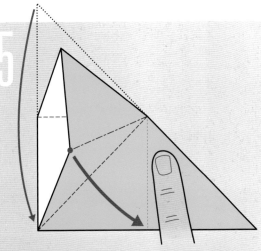

Hold the bottom of the model and then take the middle of the front left edge and pull it down to the middle of the base, then crease.

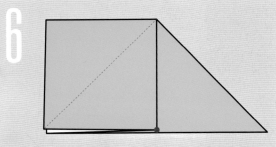

It should look like this now.

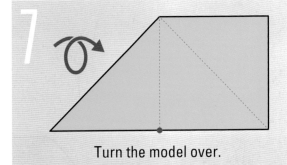

Turn the model over.

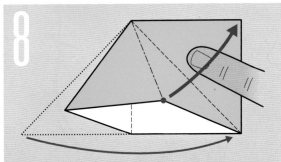

Holding the model with one hand, lift up the middle of the front bottom edge and take it to the top right corner.

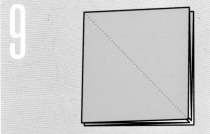

It should now look like this. This known as a 'preliminary base'.

Turn through 45° so the four points are at the bottom.

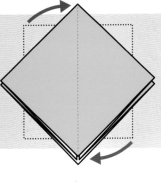

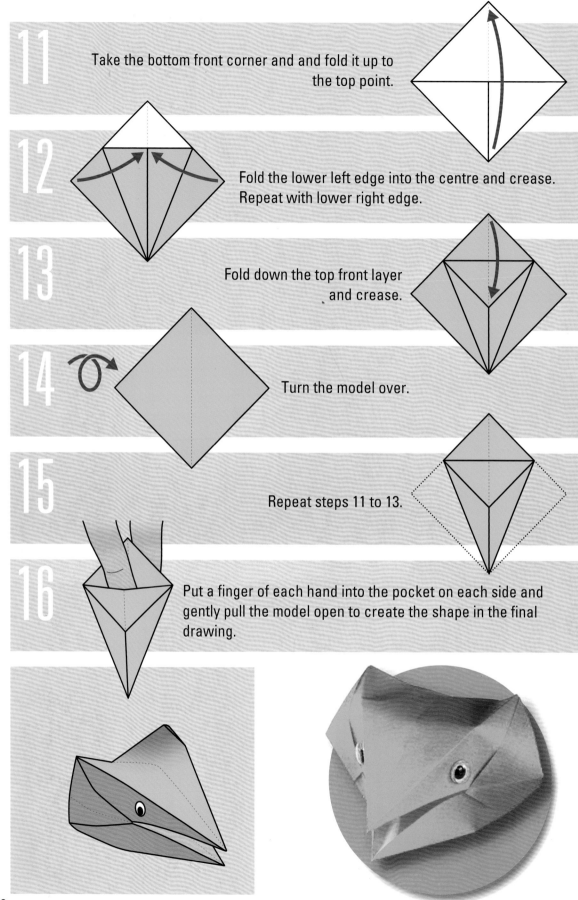

11 Take the bottom front corner and and fold it up to the top point.

12 Fold the lower left edge into the centre and crease. Repeat with lower right edge.

13 Fold down the top front layer and crease.

14 Turn the model over.

15 Repeat steps 11 to 13.

16 Put a finger of each hand into the pocket on each side and gently pull the model open to create the shape in the final drawing.

Seahorse

Start this one with the first six steps of the model seal (page 43), and then continue with the following instructions.

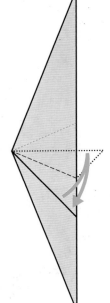

Turn the model to this position.

Fold the right half of the model behind the left and crease.

Fold up the bottom edge of the small flap to be level with the middle fold, crease and unfold.

Lift up the flap and open it up. Fold it down on the creases created in step 3.

69

Flatten as shown.

Fold, crease and unfold along the two dashed lines shown.

Now fold back and behind the two flaps created in step 6.

Fold back the point as shown. Now repeat steps 3 to 8 with the other side.

Fold the front edge back as shown. Do this on both sides.

Fold roughly along the dashed line indicated, crease and unfold. Fold the other way on the same line, crease and unfold.

Open the model a little way and make an outside reverse fold.

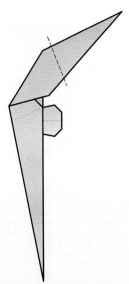

Fold roughly along the dashed line indicated, crease and unfold. Fold the other way on the same line, crease and unfold.

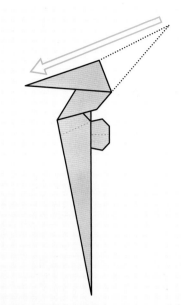

Open the model a little way and make an outside reverse fold.

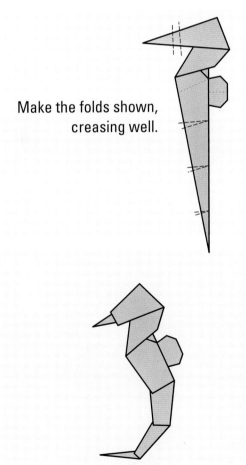

Make the folds shown, creasing well.

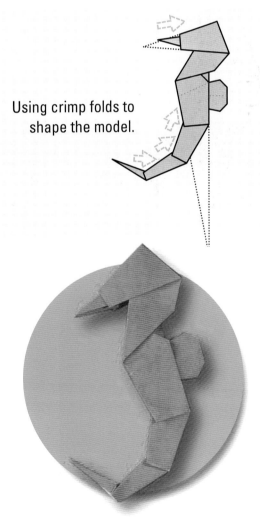

Using crimp folds to shape the model.

The finished seahorse!

Crow

To start this model follow the first 9 steps from the 'Lizard Head' (page 66) to make the preliminary base. Steps 2 to 10 on this model make what is known as a 'Bird base', and these steps will be used again in later models in the book.

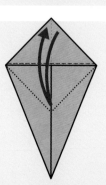

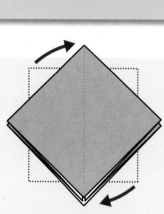

Turn through 45° so the four points are at the bottom.

Fold the lower left edge into the centre and crease. Repeat with lower right edge.

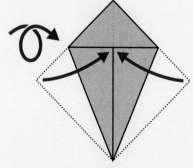

Turn the model over and repeat step 2.

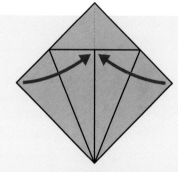

Fold the top point down and fold between the left and right points. Crease and unfold.

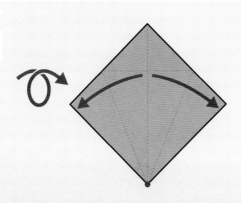

Turn the model over and unfold the two flaps.

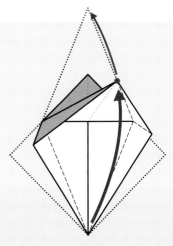

Lift up the front bottom point up as shown and fold over, creasing the centre fold and the four sides into shape.

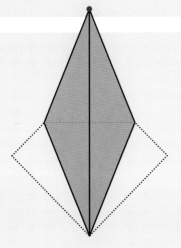

It should look like this now.

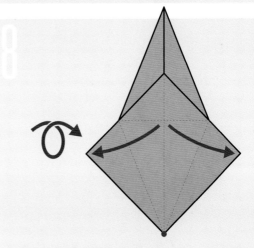

Turn the model over and open out the two flaps on this side.

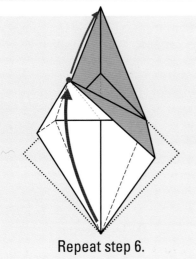

Repeat step 6.

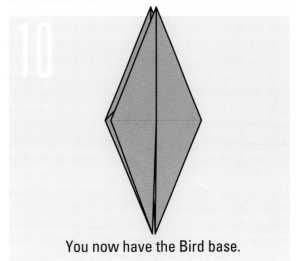

You now have the Bird base.

11

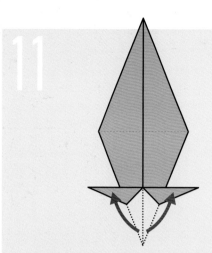

Fold up the two bottom points and crease well.

12

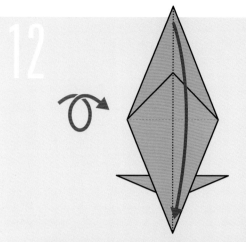

Turn over and then fold down the front top point to the bottom.

13

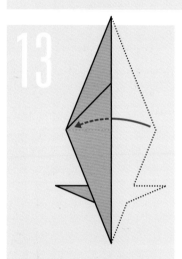

Fold in half by passing the right hand side back and behind the left.

14

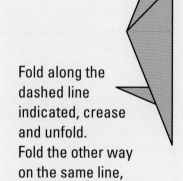

Fold along the dashed line indicated, crease and unfold.
Fold the other way on the same line, crease and unfold.

15

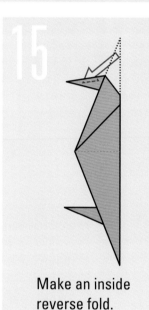

Make an inside reverse fold.

16

The completed model should look like this.

Butterfly

This model looks terrific when made of squares cut from thin, patterned wrapping paper.

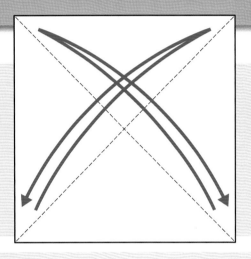

Start with a square, white side up.
Fold the bottom left corner up to the top right, crease and unfold.
Repeat with the bottom right corner up to the top left.

Fold the bottom edge up to the top one, crease and unfold.
Repeat with the right edge over to the feft one.

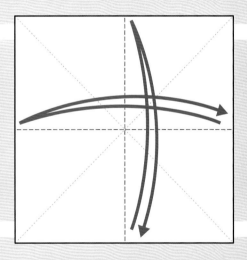

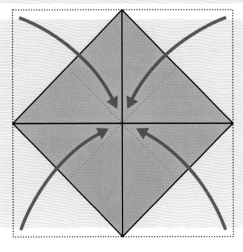

Fold the four corners into the centre and crease.

4

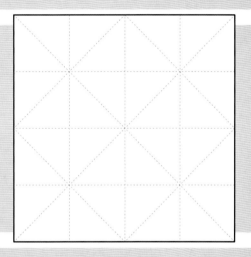

Turn the model over and fold the four corners into the centre and crease.

5

Unfold the whole sheet and place with the white side up.

6

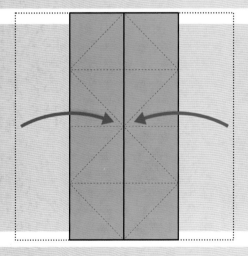

Fold both side edges into the centre.

7

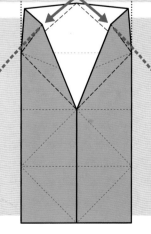

Take the two top centre points and, one at a time, pull them out in the direction of the arrows.

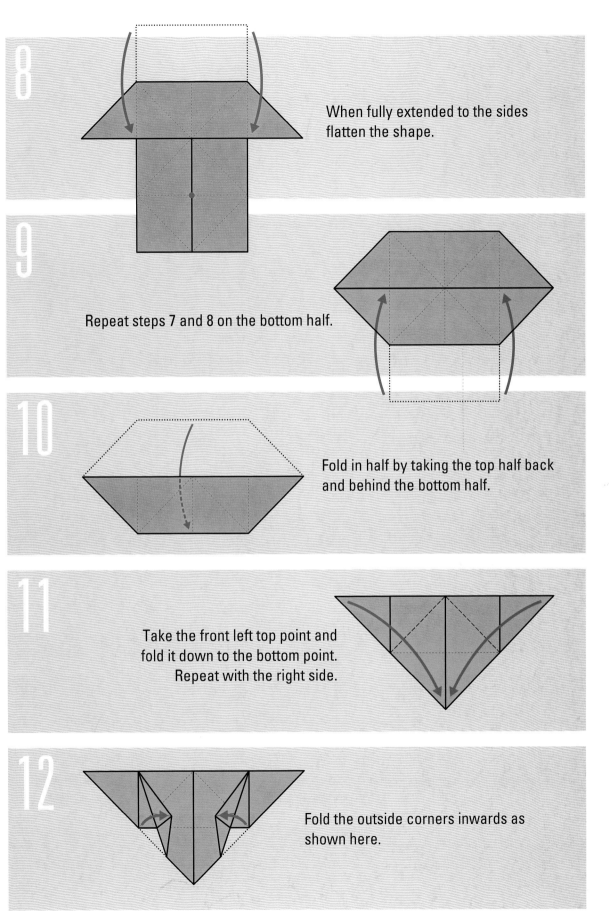

8 When fully extended to the sides flatten the shape.

9 Repeat steps 7 and 8 on the bottom half.

10 Fold in half by taking the top half back and behind the bottom half.

11 Take the front left top point and fold it down to the bottom point. Repeat with the right side.

12 Fold the outside corners inwards as shown here.

13

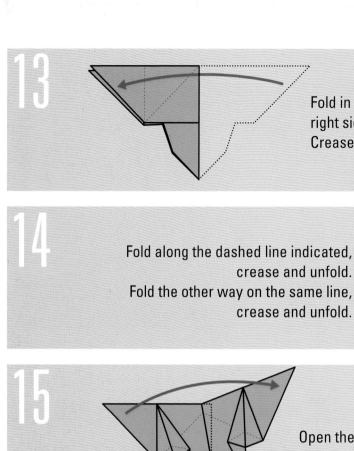

Fold in half by taking the right side over to the left. Crease well.

14

Fold along the dashed line indicated, crease and unfold.
Fold the other way on the same line, crease and unfold.

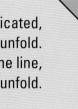

15

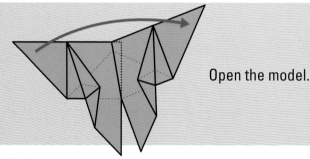

Open the model.

16

Shape the model as shown.

Horse

Start this one with the first six steps of the model seal (page 43), and then continue with the following instructions.

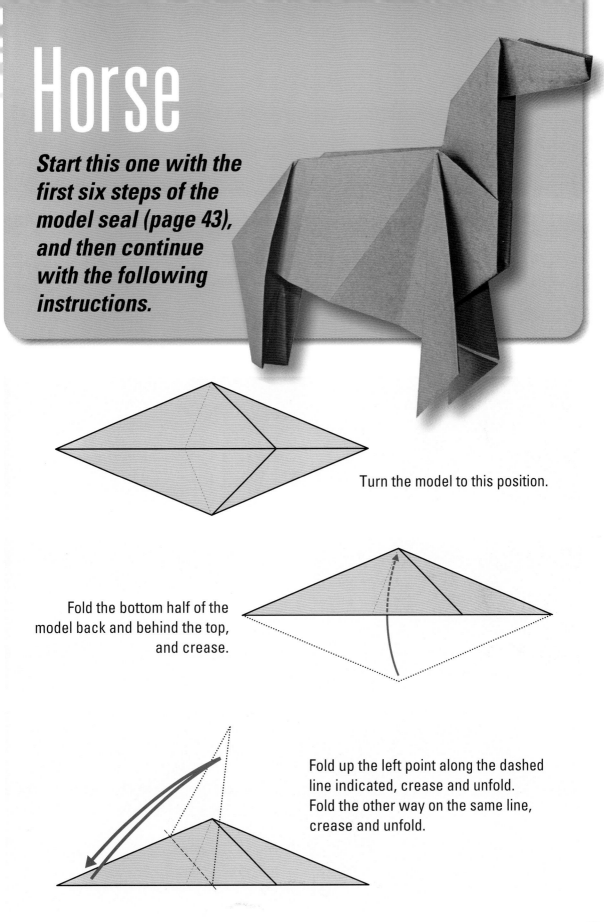

Turn the model to this position.

Fold the bottom half of the model back and behind the top, and crease.

Fold up the left point along the dashed line indicated, crease and unfold. Fold the other way on the same line, crease and unfold.

4

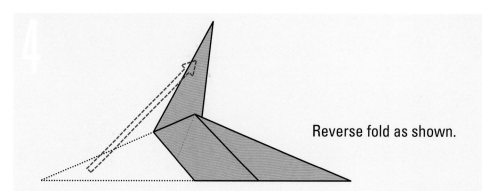

Reverse fold as shown.

5

Fold up the left point along the dashed line indicated, crease and unfold. Fold the other way on the same line, crease and unfold. Reverse fold to shape the head as in **a**. Fold and crease the nose as in **b**. Reverse fold in as shown.

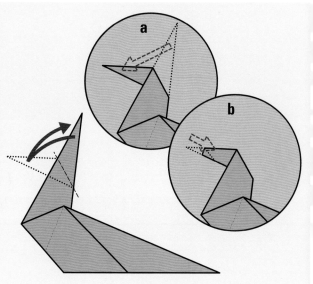

6

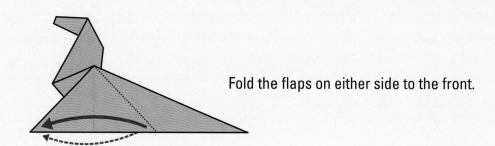

Fold the flaps on either side to the front.

7

Fold the right point along the dashed line indicated, crease and unfold. Fold the other way on the same line, crease and unfold.

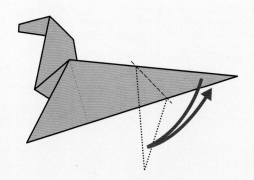

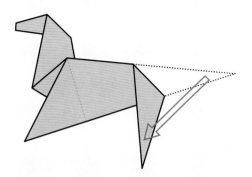

Outside reverse fold to make the back legs.

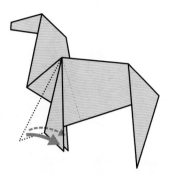

Fold the front edges of the front legs back as shown. Do this on both sides.

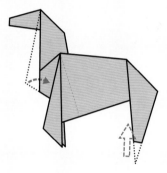

Fold inwards the front neck edges and crease well.
Fold, crease and reverse fold the bottom of the back legs as shown.

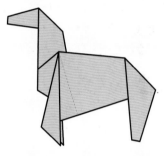

Your horse should now look like this.

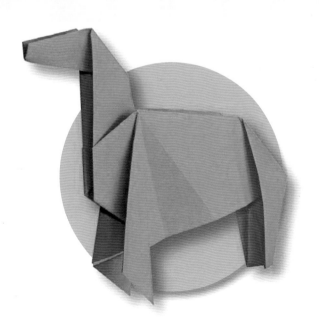

Kitten

A simple, but cute model!

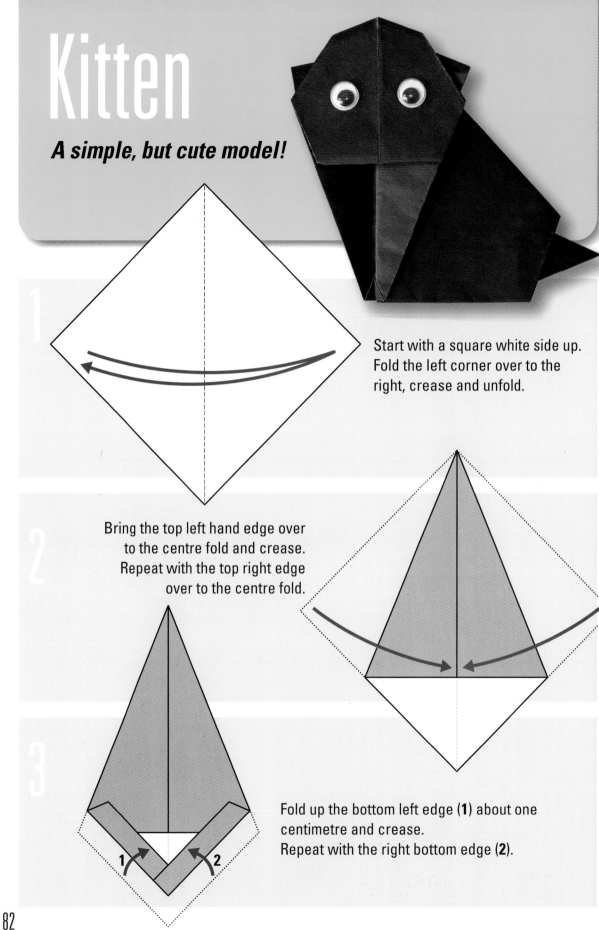

Start with a square white side up.
Fold the left corner over to the
right, crease and unfold.

Bring the top left hand edge over
to the centre fold and crease.
Repeat with the top right edge
over to the centre fold.

Fold up the bottom left edge (**1**) about one
centimetre and crease.
Repeat with the right bottom edge (**2**).

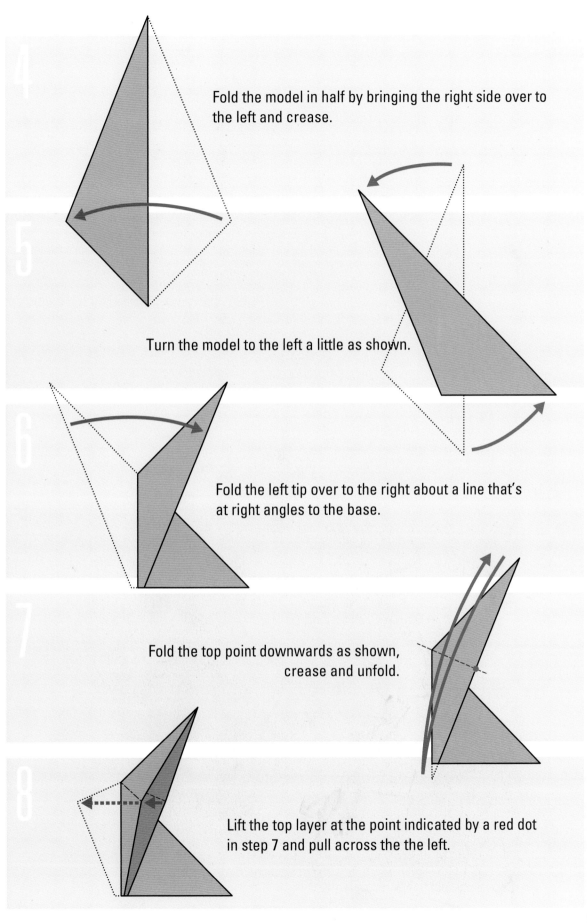

Fold the model in half by bringing the right side over to the left and crease.

Turn the model to the left a little as shown.

Fold the left tip over to the right about a line that's at right angles to the base.

Fold the top point downwards as shown, crease and unfold.

Lift the top layer at the point indicated by a red dot in step 7 and pull across the the left.

9

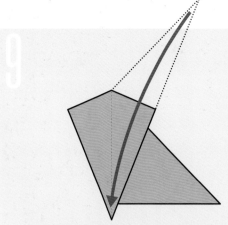

As you this the top point will want to fold down to the bottom. Fold it down, flatten and crease as shown.

10

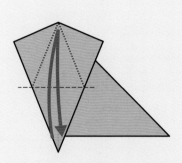

Fold up the bottom point to the top of the model, crease and fold down again.

11

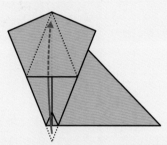

Fold the last fold backwards inside the head and crease.

12

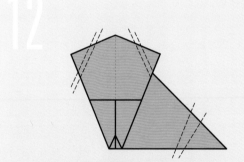

To create the ears and tail fold and crease along the six dashed lines indicated.

13

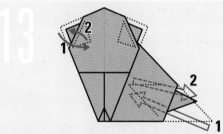

In each case fold back on the inner crease and fold out on the outer one. Crease well.

14

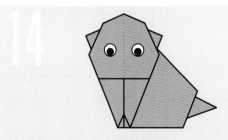

Add eyes to complete the model.

84

Flapping Duck

A fun model that flaps its wings when you pull its tail!

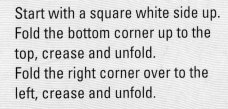

1

Start with a square white side up.
Fold the bottom corner up to the top, crease and unfold.
Fold the right corner over to the left, crease and unfold.

2

Turn the sheet over and fold the left, right and bottom corners to the centre.
Fold the top corner to the centre of the other side.

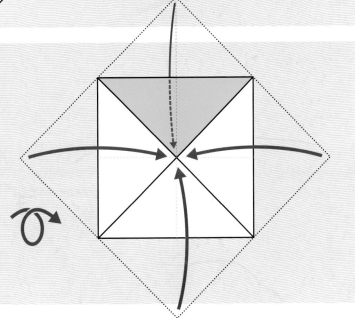

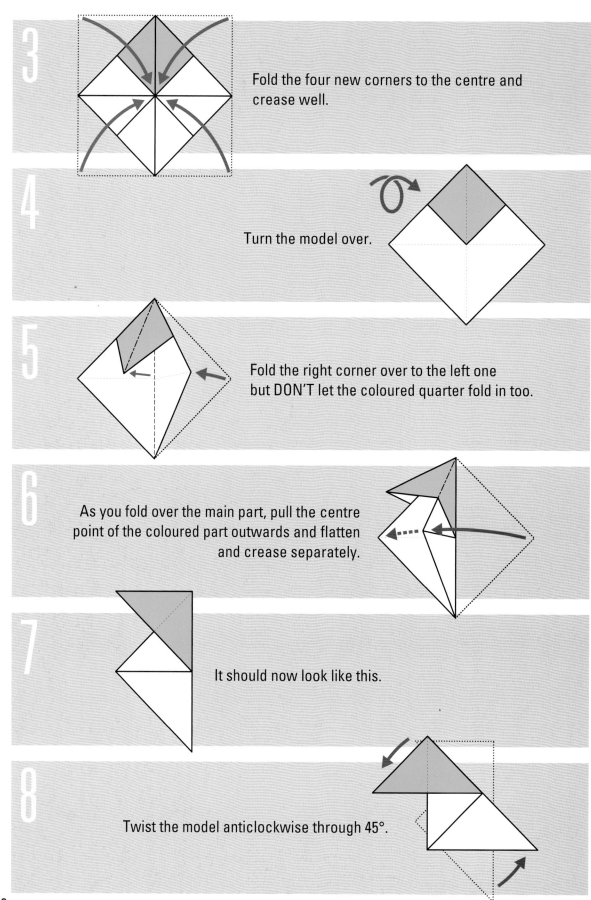

3 Fold the four new corners to the centre and crease well.

4 Turn the model over.

5 Fold the right corner over to the left one but DON'T let the coloured quarter fold in too.

6 As you fold over the main part, pull the centre point of the coloured part outwards and flatten and crease separately.

7 It should now look like this.

8 Twist the model anticlockwise through 45°.

9

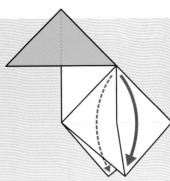

Fold down the white flaps on each side.

10

Holding the head with the left hand, pull the white part away to the right as indicated.

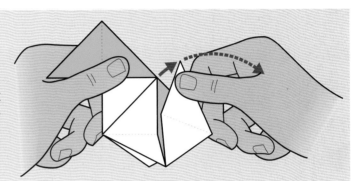

11

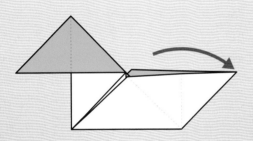

As you do this, the two bottom points will come up again.
When the tail is back as far as it will go, flatten the model and crease.

12

Bring the point at the back of the head forward and then find the white corner (shown by a red dot) and pull it down. Crease the diagonal fold the other way (indicated by black arrow) and flatten.

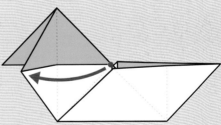

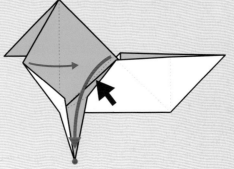

13

Your model should now look like this.

14

Turn the model over and repeat step 12 on the other side.

15

Hold the model as shown and when the tail is pulled the wings will flap!

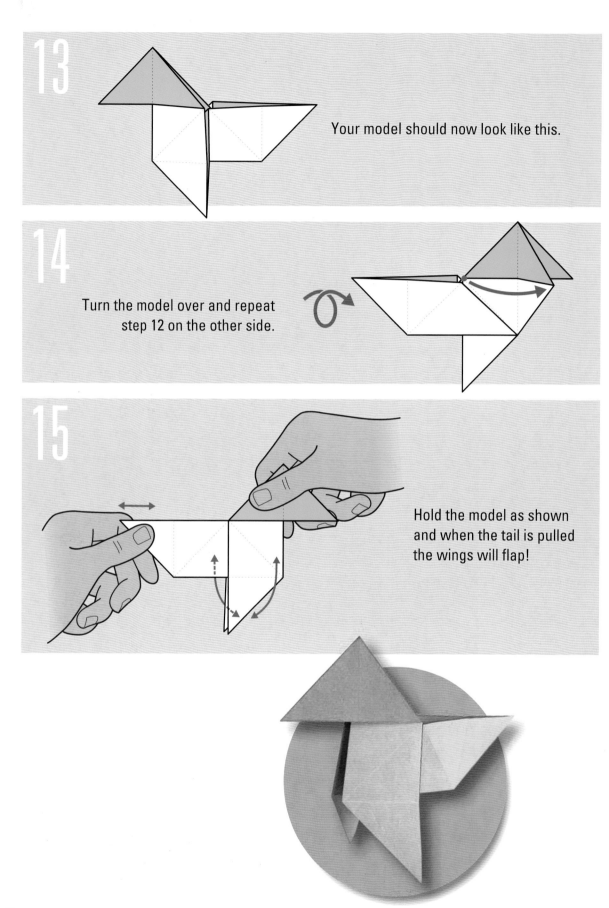

Fish

This model requires the use of a pair of scissors.

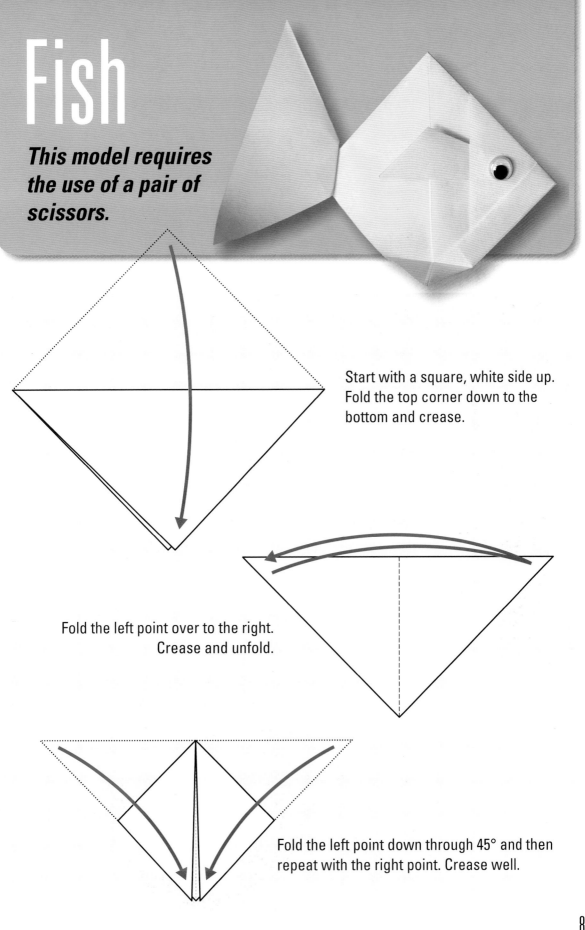

Start with a square, white side up. Fold the top corner down to the bottom and crease.

Fold the left point over to the right. Crease and unfold.

Fold the left point down through 45° and then repeat with the right point. Crease well.

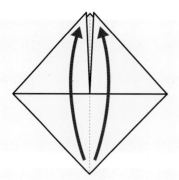

Fold the two front points at the bottom up to the top corner. Crease well.

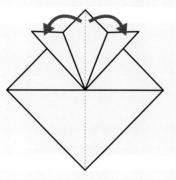

Fold the two front points, now at top, outwards as shown.

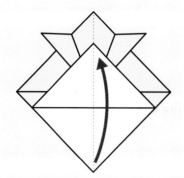

The bottom corner now has two layers. Fold up and crease the top one to the position shown.

Now fold the bottom edge of this flap along a line on the centre of the model and crease.

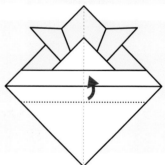

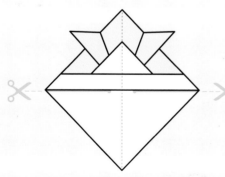

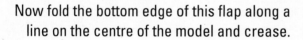

Cut into the bottom flap from each side corner to about 6 or 7 millimetres from the centre.

Carefully fold this flap back behind the model.

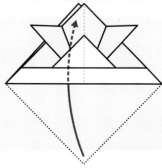

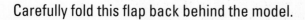

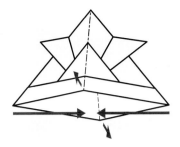

Open up the model by pulling the front and back apart and pushing in the two side points.

Flatten and crease.

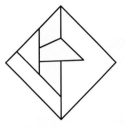

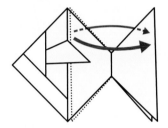

Pull the tail back, turning inside out and flattening at the join.

Fold up and crease the bottom of the body and curve out and up the bottom points of the tail.

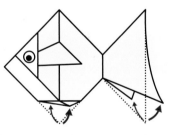

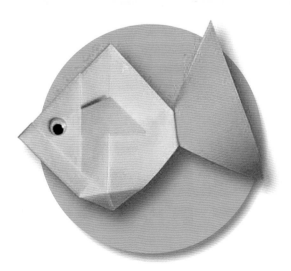

Swan

Use a white sheet of paper to make this elegant model of a swan.

Fold the bottom corner up to the top, crease and unfold.

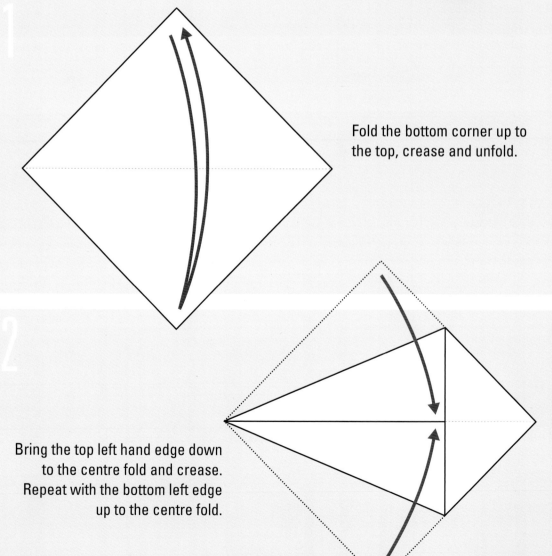

Bring the top left hand edge down to the centre fold and crease. Repeat with the bottom left edge up to the centre fold.

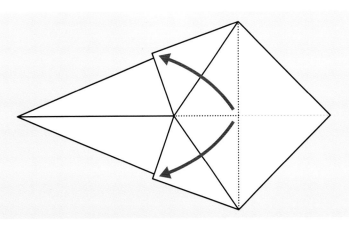

Fold the two inner points out to the positions shown and crease.

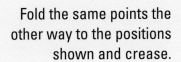
Fold the same points the other way to the positions shown and crease.
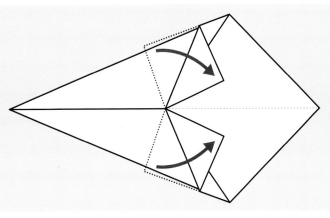

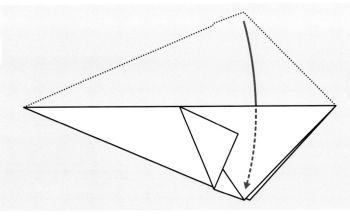

Fold the top half back and behind the bottom half.

Fold along the dashed lines indicated, crease and unfold. Fold the other way on the same lines, crease and unfold.

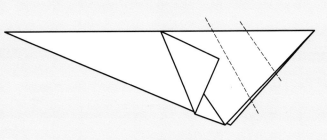

7

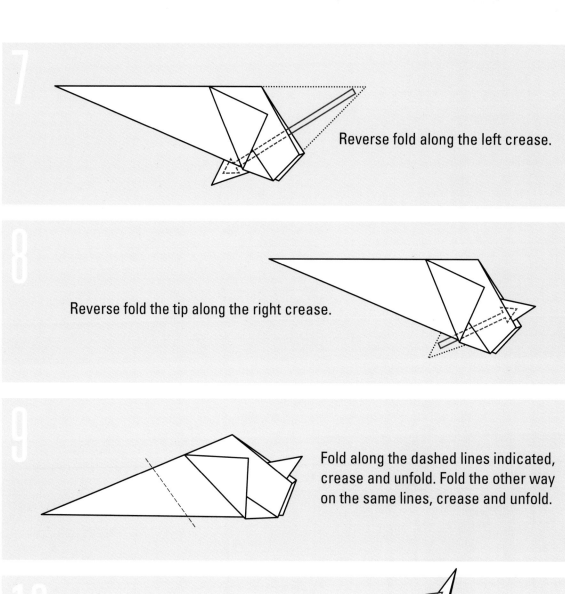

Reverse fold along the left crease.

8

Reverse fold the tip along the right crease.

9

Fold along the dashed lines indicated, crease and unfold. Fold the other way on the same lines, crease and unfold.

10

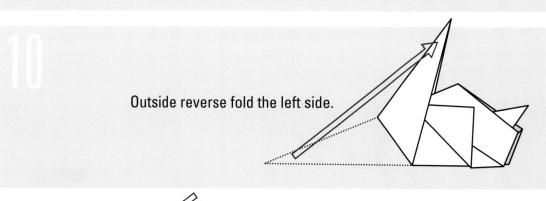

Outside reverse fold the left side.

11

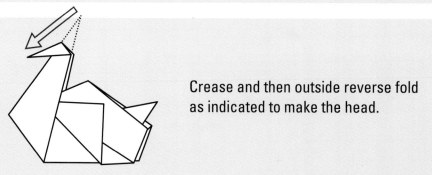

Crease and then outside reverse fold as indicated to make the head.

12

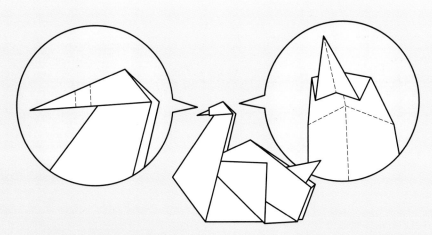

Double crease the head as shown on the left picture and open up the head and fold as shown on the right.
Then fold the head up again.

13

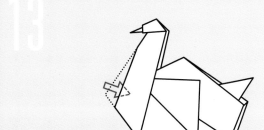

Forward and backward crease down the front of the neck at the place indicated in step 13, and then inside reverse fold the flap.

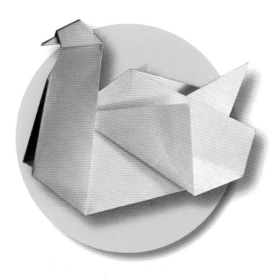

Mouse

Start this one with the first six steps of the model seal (page 43), and then continue with the following instructions.

1

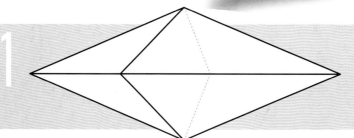

Position the model as shown here.

2

Turn the model over. Then fold the left point over until the fold will be directly over the two points underneath. Crease.

3

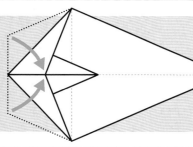

Fold in the two left points as shown, and crease.

4

Turn the model over. Fold the outside edge of the front bottom flap as shown.

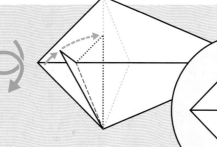

5

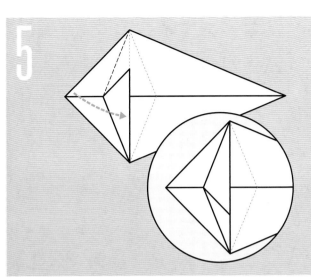

Fold the outside edge of the front top flap as shown.

6

Fold the top half of the model back and behind the front half.

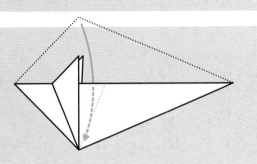

7

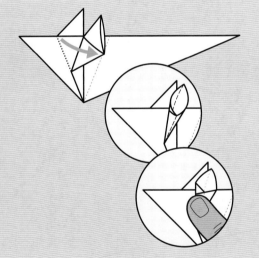

Fold and crease the the flap back as shown in the first diagram.
Open the top part with a small finger or blunt pencil.
Flatten and shape as shown.

8

Fold along the dashed line indicated, crease and unfold.
Fold the other way on the same line, crease and unfold.

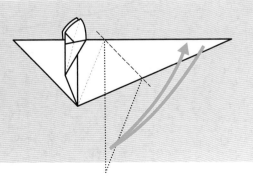

9

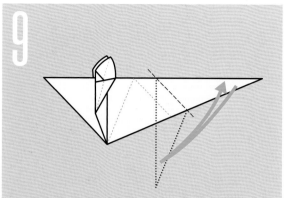

Repeat step 8 along another line about a centimetre to the right of the first.

10

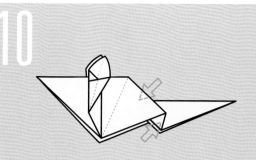

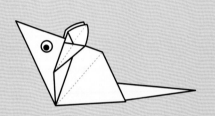

Repeat step 8 along another line about a centimetre to the right of the first. Then reverse fold as shown.

11

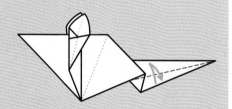

Fold up the bottom half of the tail. Open the tail and then fold in each side. Crease well.

12

Add some eyes and your little mouse is complete.

Sheep

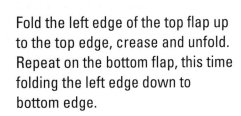

Take care!
The models are now
starting to get a little
more difficult.

Start with a square, coloured
side up.
Fold the right corner over to the
left, crease and unfold.
Fold the bottom corner up to the
top, crease and unfold.

Fold the top point over to the
centre and crease.
Repeat with the bottom point.

Fold the left edge of the top flap up
to the top edge, crease and unfold.
Repeat on the bottom flap, this time
folding the left edge down to
bottom edge.

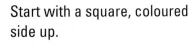

99

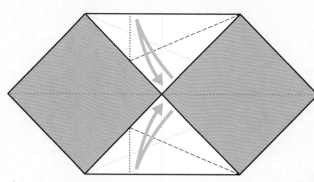

Repeat step 3 actions with the same flaps but this time folding the right edges.

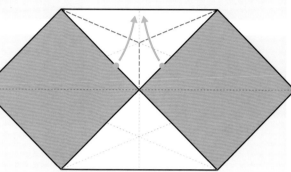

Fold over the two bottom edges of the top flap, along the red dashed lines, until they lay on the top edge. The bottom corner of the flap will now point upwards. Flatten neatly to the left and crease, and then to the right and crease.

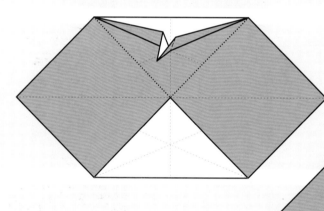

The bottom corner of the flap will now point upwards.

Flatten neatly to the left and crease.

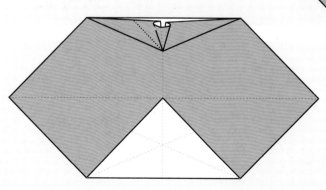

Raise the flap and open with a little finger or a blunt pencil.

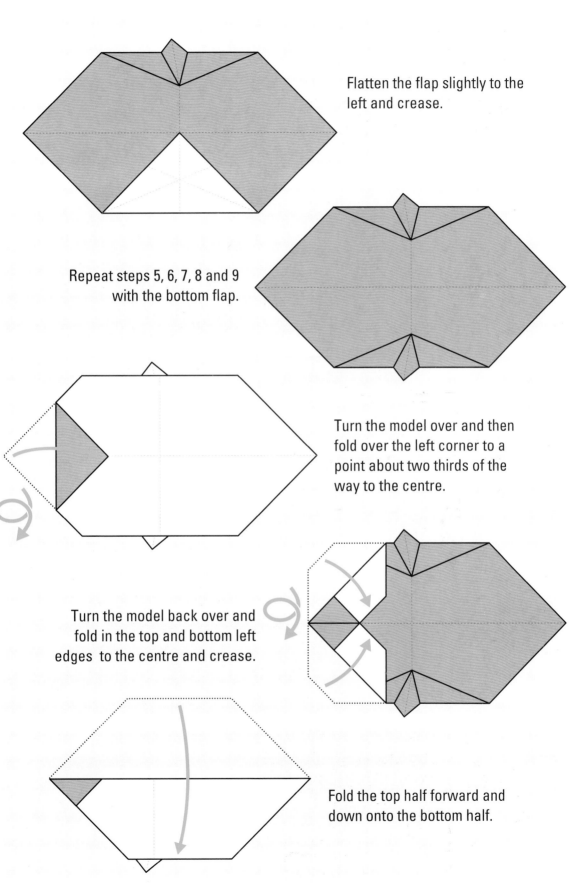

Flatten the flap slightly to the left and crease.

Repeat steps 5, 6, 7, 8 and 9 with the bottom flap.

Turn the model over and then fold over the left corner to a point about two thirds of the way to the centre.

Turn the model back over and fold in the top and bottom left edges to the centre and crease.

Fold the top half forward and down onto the bottom half.

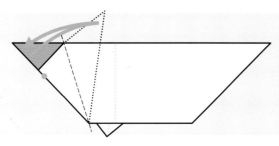

Fold, crease and unfold the left point about the dashed lines indicated.

Lift the top part and take to the point indicated.

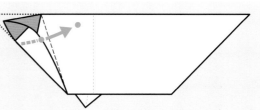

Flatten and crease.

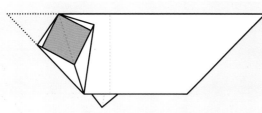

Fold down and crease the top corner of the coloured square.
Fold the the bottom corner and crease behind.

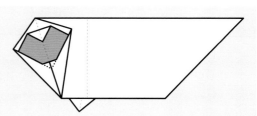

Fold the left half of the face back and behind the right and crease well.

Hold the model with your right hand in the position as shown.
Hold the face with your left and pull out to the position shown and flatten.

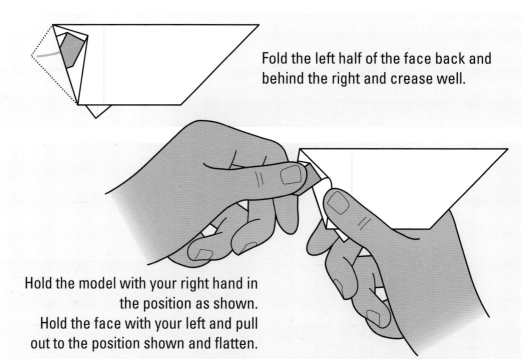

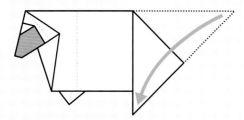

Fold down as shown, crease and unfold. Fold the other way on the same fold, crease and unfold.

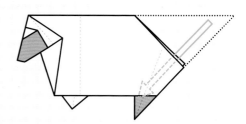

Inside reverse fold to make the back feet.

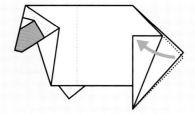

Fold over the rear edge as shown and crease and unfold. Repeat the fold and crease in the other direction. Repeat with the other side.

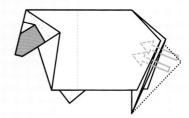

Inside reverse fold both folds.

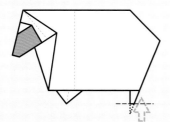

Fold and crease the bottom part of the back foot. Unfold and inside reverse fold to complete the model.

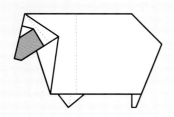

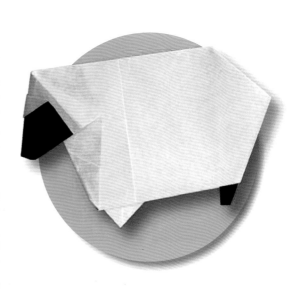

Dolphin

Crease this model well as you go along because some of the folds get quite thick.

1

Start with a square, white side up.
Fold the bottom left corner up to the top right,
crease and unfold.
Repeat with the bottom right corner up
to the top left.

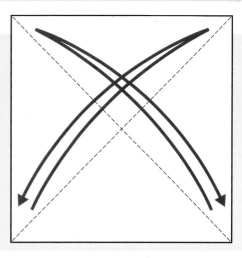

2

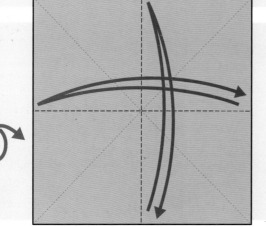

Turn the sheet over and fold the
bottom edge up to the top one,
crease and unfold.
Repeat with the right edge over
to the left one.

3

Turn the sheet back over and fold the top
right corner down to the bottom left one.

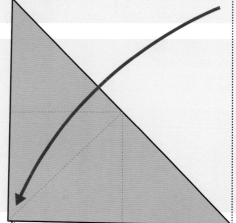

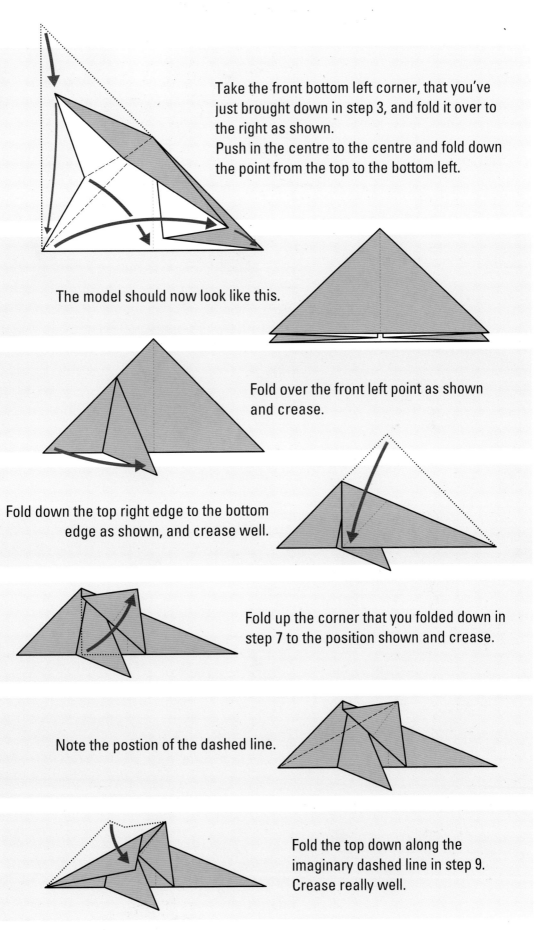

4 Take the front bottom left corner, that you've just brought down in step 3, and fold it over to the right as shown.
Push in the centre to the centre and fold down the point from the top to the bottom left.

5 The model should now look like this.

6 Fold over the front left point as shown and crease.

7 Fold down the top right edge to the bottom edge as shown, and crease well.

8 Fold up the corner that you folded down in step 7 to the position shown and crease.

9 Note the postion of the dashed line.

10 Fold the top down along the imaginary dashed line in step 9. Crease really well.

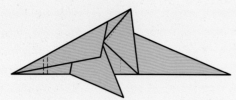

Note the position of the two dashed lines.

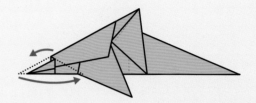

Fold over on the right line and then back again on the left one. Crease well.

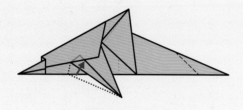

Fold up the lower edge of the fin and crease.

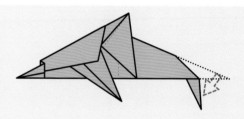

Crease both ways on the dashed line shown on the tail in step 13 Inside reverse fold.

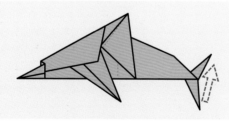

Pull out the centre part of the tail and crease into position.

 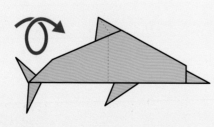

Turn the model over to reveal the finished model. This looks good stuck to a square of different coloured card.

Flapping Bird

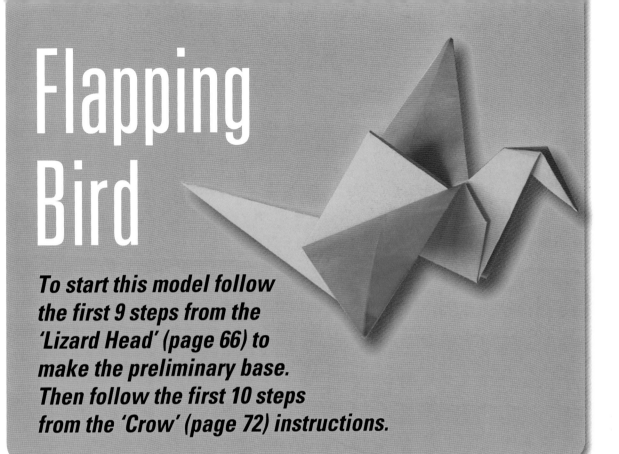

To start this model follow the first 9 steps from the 'Lizard Head' (page 66) to make the preliminary base. Then follow the first 10 steps from the 'Crow' (page 72) instructions.

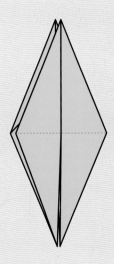

Start with the bird base as shown here.

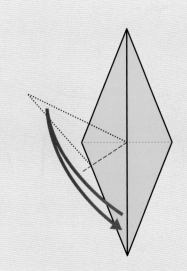

Fold along the dashed line indicated, crease and unfold. Fold the other way on the same line, crease and unfold.

3

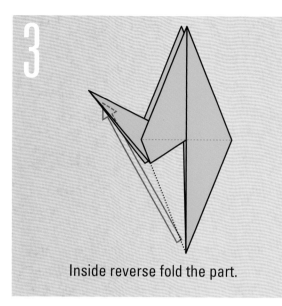

Inside reverse fold the part.

4

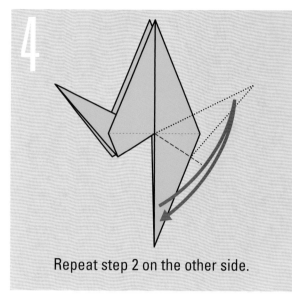

Repeat step 2 on the other side.

5

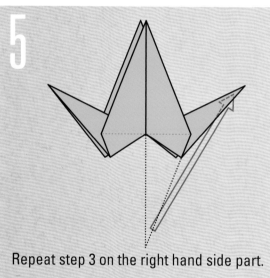

Repeat step 3 on the right hand side part.

6

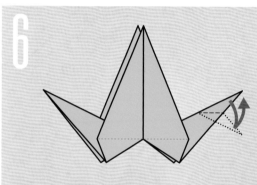

Fold along the dashed line indicated, crease and unfold.
Fold the other way on the same line, crease and unfold.

7

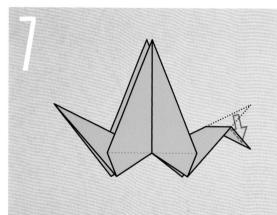

Inside reverse fold the part to create the head.

8

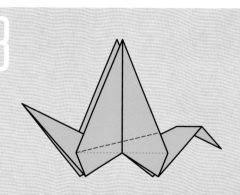

Note the postion of the dashed line on the right wing.

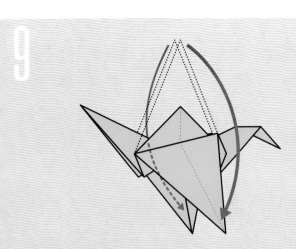

Fold down the wing and crease.
Repeat with the left wing.

10

To make your model flap its
wings hold the front of the
bird with your right hand as
shown and pull the tail with
the left hand.

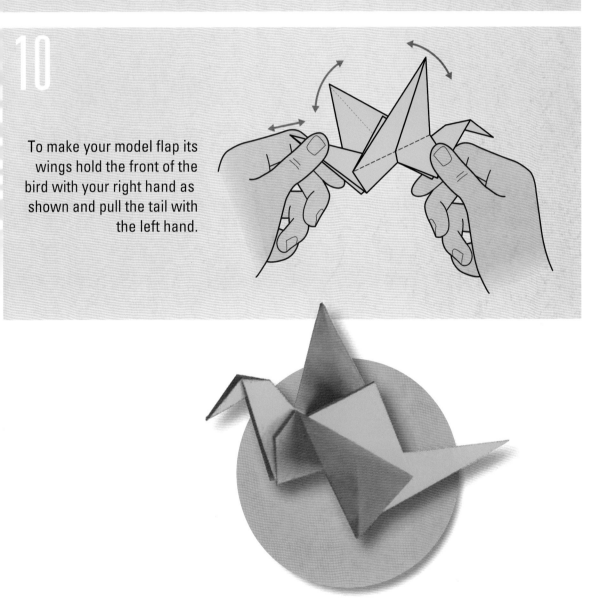

Rabbit

To start this little rabbit follow the first 9 steps from the 'Lizard Head' (page 66) to make the prelimanary base. Then follow the first 10 steps from the 'Crow' (page 72) instructions.

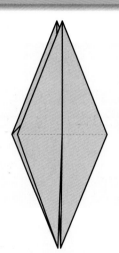

Start with the bird base as shown here.

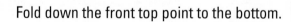

Fold down the front top point to the bottom.

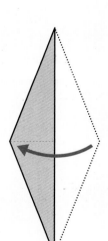

Fold the model in half by bringing the right forward and over the left side.

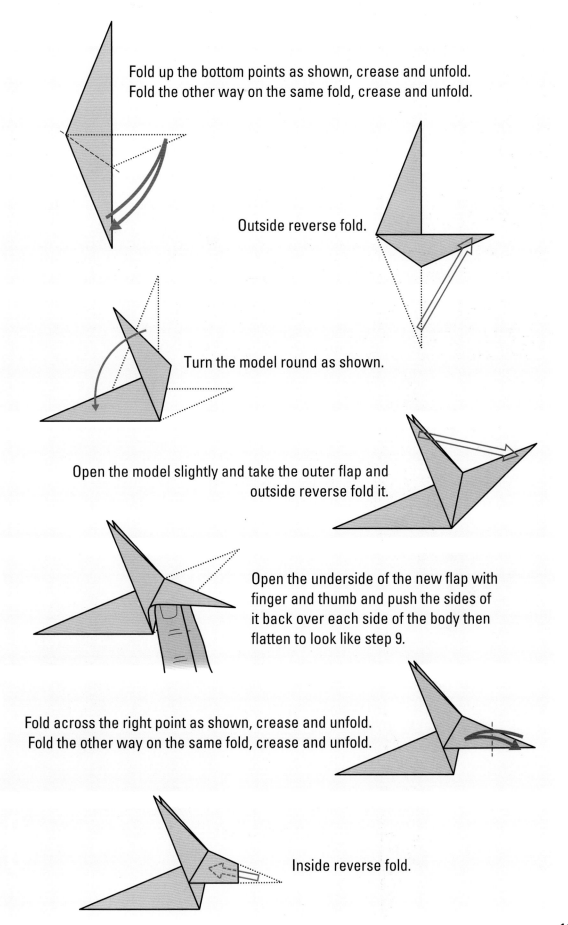

Fold up the bottom points as shown, crease and unfold.
Fold the other way on the same fold, crease and unfold.

Outside reverse fold.

Turn the model round as shown.

Open the model slightly and take the outer flap and
outside reverse fold it.

Open the underside of the new flap with
finger and thumb and push the sides of
it back over each side of the body then
flatten to look like step 9.

Fold across the right point as shown, crease and unfold.
Fold the other way on the same fold, crease and unfold.

Inside reverse fold.

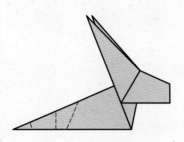

Fold, crease and unfold along the three lines shown here.

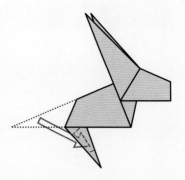

Inside reverse fold along the right fold.

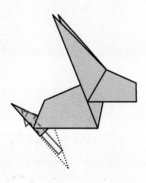

Inside reverse fold along the next.

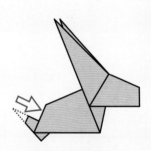

Inside reverse fold the last one.

Open up the ears to complete the model.

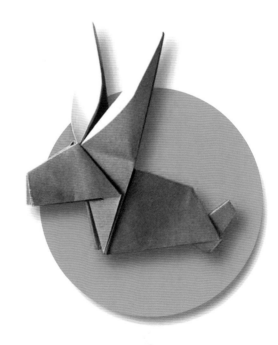

Inflatable Goldfish

This model may need a bit of puff to blow it up!

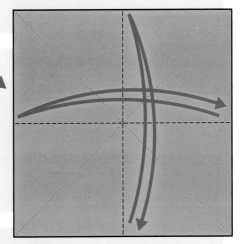

1

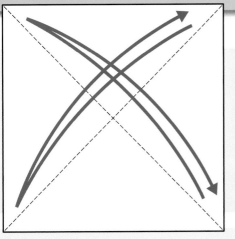

Start with a square, white side up.
Fold the bottom left corner up to the top right, crease and unfold.
Repeat with the bottom right corner up to the top left.

2

Turn the sheet over and fold the bottom edge up to the top one, crease and unfold. Repeat with the right edge over to the left one.

3

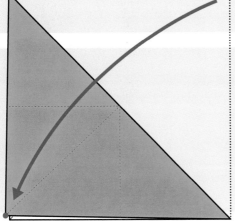

Fold the top right corner down to the bottom left one.

113

4

Hold the bottom right triangle and then take the top point, at bottom left, across to bottom right.
Push in the centre of the left side as shown and flatten.

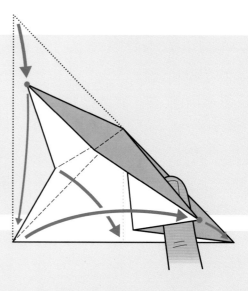

5

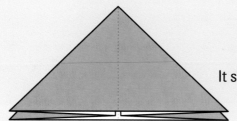

It should look like this now.

6

Fold up the front left point and crease.
Repeat with the front right point.

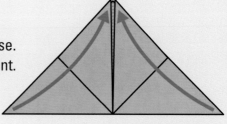

7

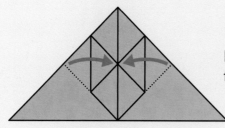

Fold in the left and right points of the two small flaps to the centre.

8

Fold down the left and right front top points down to the centre.

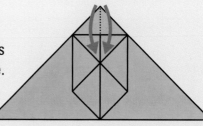

9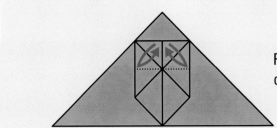

Fold, crease and unfold the two flaps created in step 8 as shown.

10

Open the small pockets at the top of the small side triangles and insert the flaps made in step 9. Flatten.

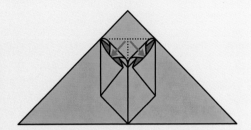

11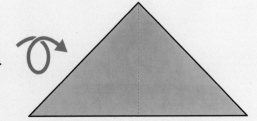

It should now look like this.

12

Turn the model over.

13

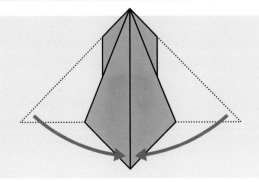

Fold the left edge into the centre and repeat with the right side.

14 Take the bottom left point over as shown, fold and crease.

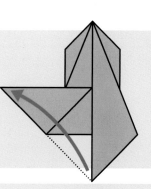

15 Fold over the top of the left side.

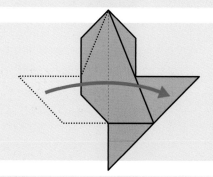

16 Holding the tail, blow into the main body at the point shown.
You may need to slightly open a hole with a pencil.

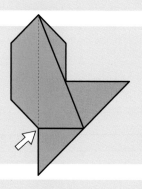

17 You may need to blow a few times to fully inflate it.

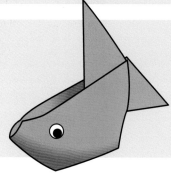

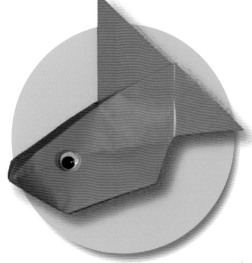

Snake

Here's a model that's a bit different.

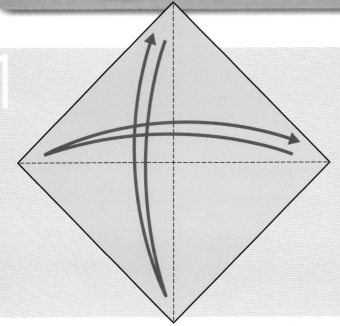

Start with a square, coloured side up, and fold the top corner down to the bottom, crease and unfold.
Fold the right corner over to the left one, crease and unfold.

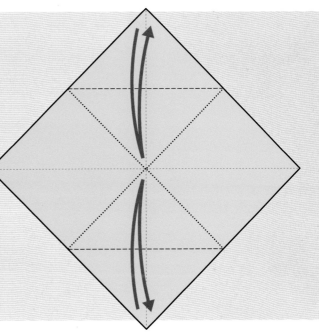

Fold down the top corner to the centre, crease and unfold. Repeat with the bottom corner up to the centre and unfold.

117

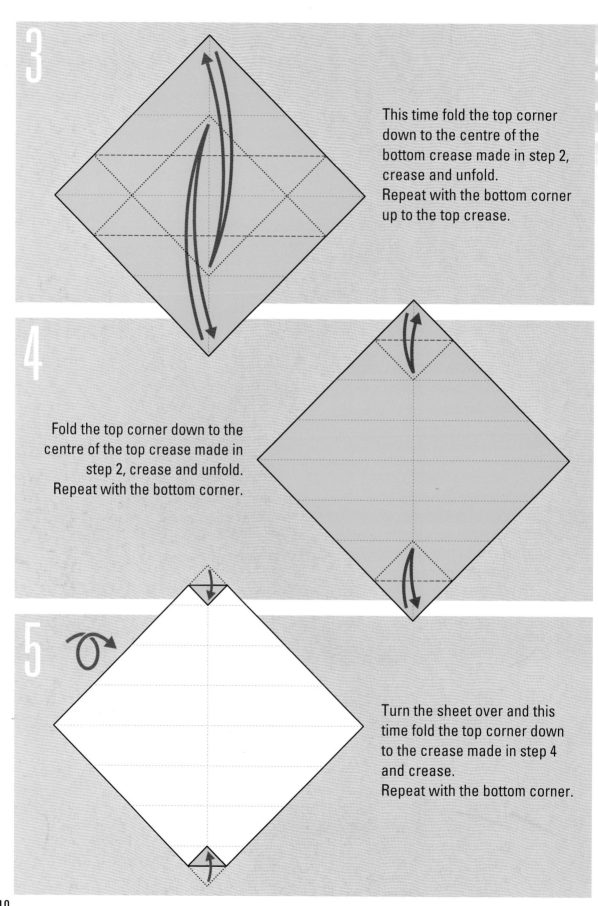

3

This time fold the top corner down to the centre of the bottom crease made in step 2, crease and unfold.
Repeat with the bottom corner up to the top crease.

4

Fold the top corner down to the centre of the top crease made in step 2, crease and unfold.
Repeat with the bottom corner.

5

Turn the sheet over and this time fold the top corner down to the crease made in step 4 and crease.
Repeat with the bottom corner.

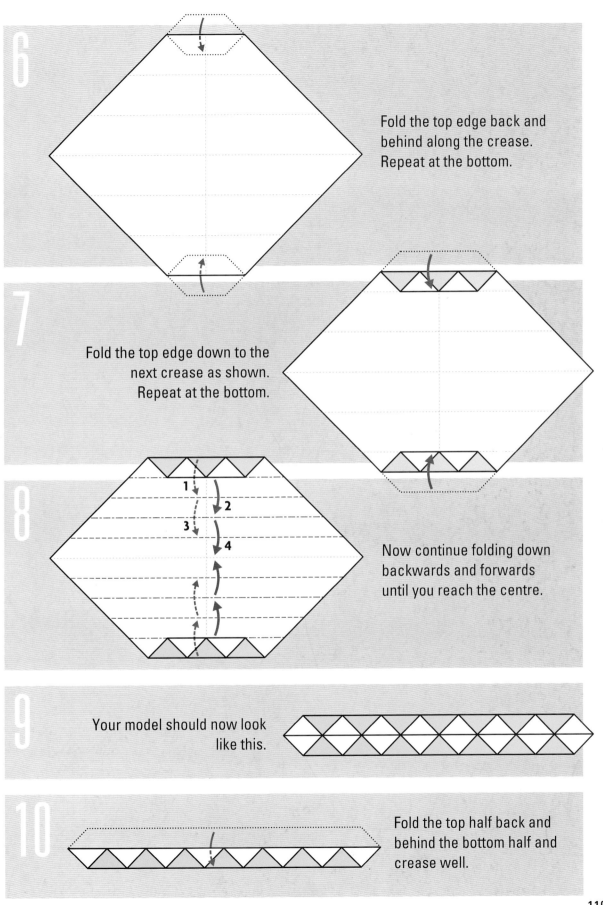

6 Fold the top edge back and behind along the crease. Repeat at the bottom.

7 Fold the top edge down to the next crease as shown. Repeat at the bottom.

8 1 2 3 4

Now continue folding down backwards and forwards until you reach the centre.

9 Your model should now look like this.

10 Fold the top half back and behind the bottom half and crease well.

11

Fold along the dashed line as shown, crease and unfold.
Fold the other way on the same fold, crease and unfold.

12

Outside reverse fold.

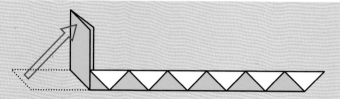

13

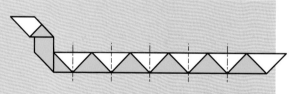

Fold along the dashed line as shown, crease and unfold.
Fold the other way on the same fold, crease and unfold.

14

Outside reverse fold.

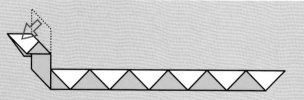

15

Fold alternate mountain and valley folds
along the body as shown.

16

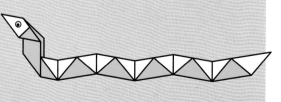

Add eyes and your snake is ready to
slither away!

Inflatable Rabbit

Start the model by following steps 1 to 12 from the 'Inflatable Goldfish' (page 113) then continue with step 1 here.

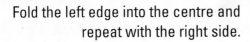

You have just turned the model over and it now looks like this.

Fold the left edge into the centre and repeat with the right side.

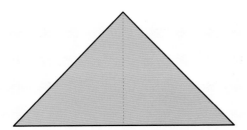

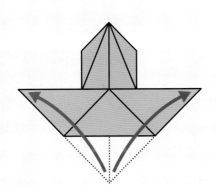

Fold the left bottom point up and out as shown, and crease.
Repeat with the right side.

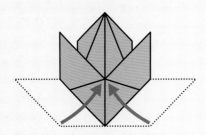

Fold the bottom left edge through 45° to the centre as shown. Repeat with the right side.

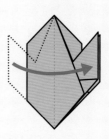

Fold the front half of the left side over and crease.

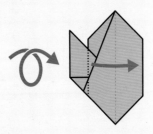

Turn the model over and then fold the front part of the left side over to the right.

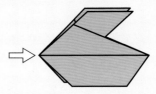

Holding an ear in each hand, with the nose end facing you (shown with the white arrow), blow into the nose until the body is inflated. You may need to blow a few times to fully inflate it.

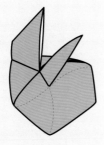

The finished model will look like this.

Dinosaur

To start this model follow the first 9 steps from the 'Lizard Head' (page 66) to make the preliminary base.
Then follow the first 10 steps from the 'Crow' (page 72) instructions.

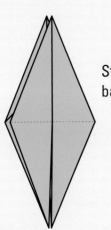

1

Start with the bird base as shown here.

2

Fold the front top point down to the bottom.

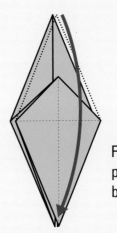

3

Fold the model in half by bringing the right side forward and over the left.

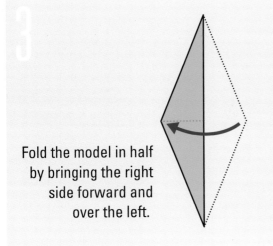

4

Fold up the front bottom point as shown.

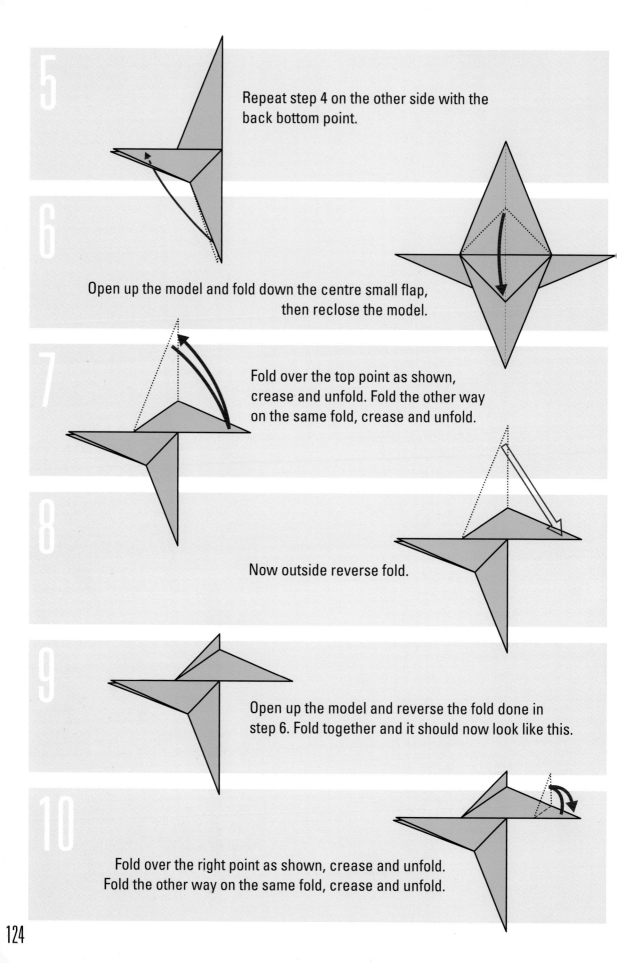

5 Repeat step 4 on the other side with the back bottom point.

6 Open up the model and fold down the centre small flap, then reclose the model.

7 Fold over the top point as shown, crease and unfold. Fold the other way on the same fold, crease and unfold.

8 Now outside reverse fold.

9 Open up the model and reverse the fold done in step 6. Fold together and it should now look like this.

10 Fold over the right point as shown, crease and unfold. Fold the other way on the same fold, crease and unfold.

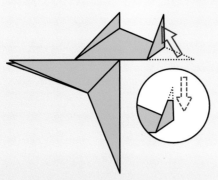

Outside reverse fold to create the head. Then inside reverse fold the nose as shown in the inset.

Inside reverse fold the part as shown.

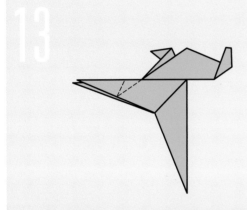

Fold and crease each leg along the two dashed lines indicated.

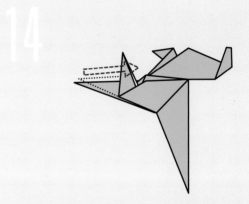

Inside reverse each leg as shown.

The final model should look like this.

Owl

To start this model follow the first 9 steps from the 'Lizard Head' (page 66) to make the preliminary base.
Then follow the first 10 steps from the 'Crow' (page 72) instructions.

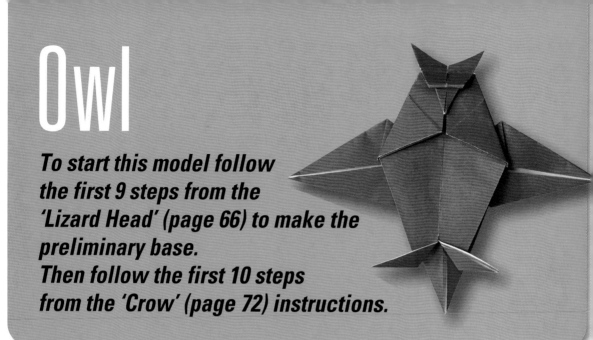

1

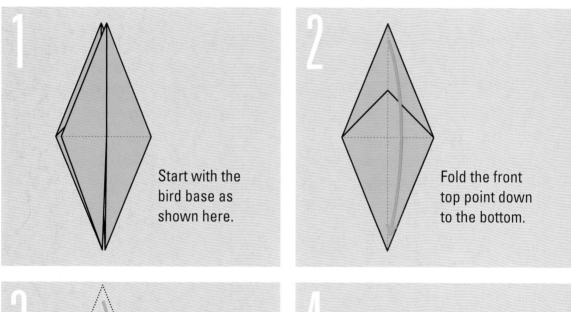

Start with the bird base as shown here.

2

Fold the front top point down to the bottom.

3

Turn the model over and fold down the top point.

4

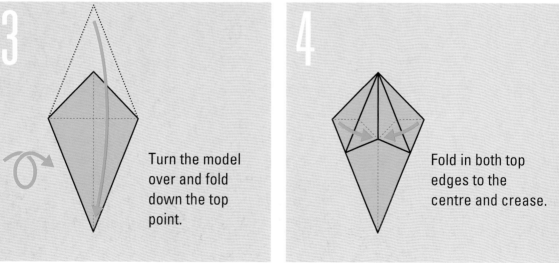

Fold in both top edges to the centre and crease.

5

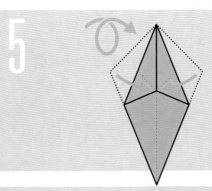

Turn the model over and fold in the two top edges to the centre, like step 4.

6

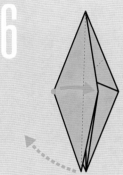

7

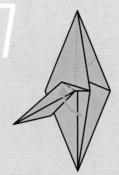

8

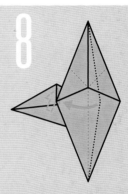

Lift the front left flap indicated by the blue dot and pull to the right.
Take the bottom point and pull up to the left to the position shown and flatten.

9

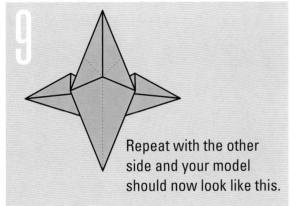

Repeat with the other side and your model should now look like this.

10

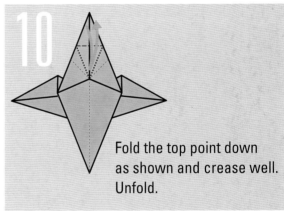

Fold the top point down as shown and crease well. Unfold.

11

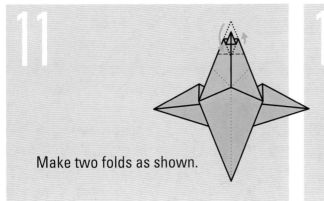

Make two folds as shown.

12

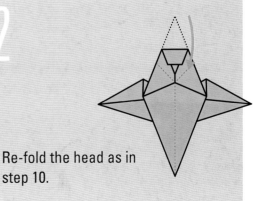

Re-fold the head as in step 10.

13

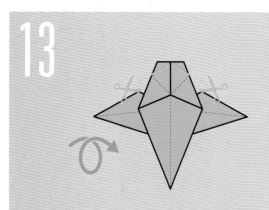

Turn the model over and cut across the top layer on each side as indicated.

14

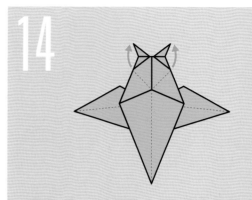

Lift up the flaps to create the ears.

15

Turn over and cut up the middle of the front point as shown.

16

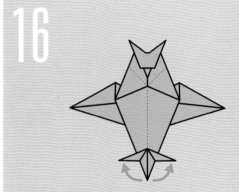

Fold up the points as shown to create the feet.

17

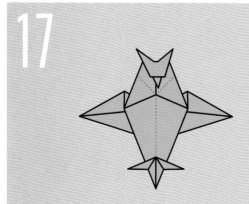

The final model should look like this.

Little dog

A lovely model but quite difficult to make.

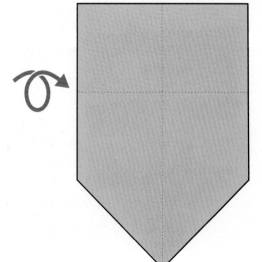

Start with a square, white side up. Fold the top corner down to the bottom, crease and unfold. Repeat with the right corner over to the left.

Fold the top, left and right corners into the centre and crease.

Turn the model over.

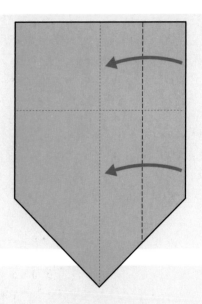

Fold the right hand edge over to the centre, folding out the right flap from behind before you crease.

It should look like this now.

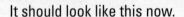

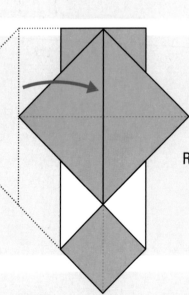

Repeat step 4 with the left side.

Put your finger under the small pocket at the top and push over to the left. When you get to position shown flatten the part.
Repeat with the right top pocket.

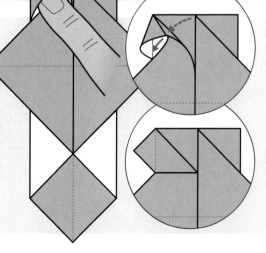

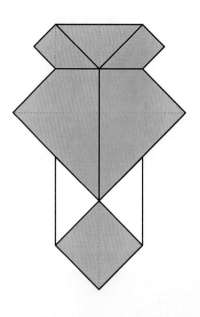

It should look like this now.

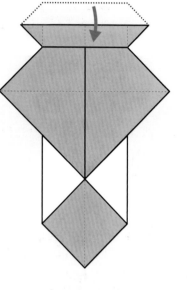

Fold the top half of the newly created part forward and down as shown and crease.

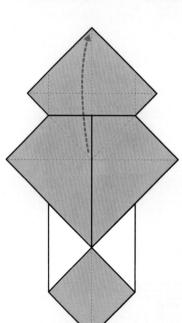

Lift up the flap from behind.

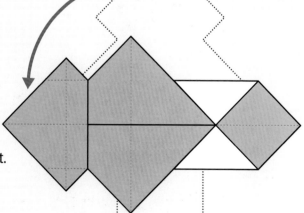

Turn the model through 90° to the left.

Now turn the model over.

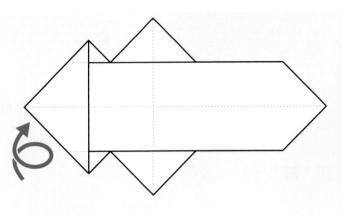

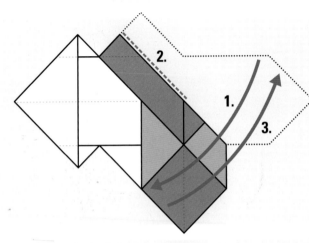

1. Diagonally fold over the area shown as shaded here.
2. Only crease this part of the fold.
3. Unfold.

Repeat with the other side and this should be how it looks.

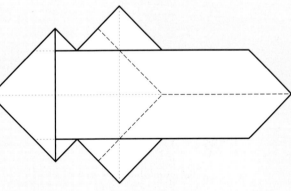

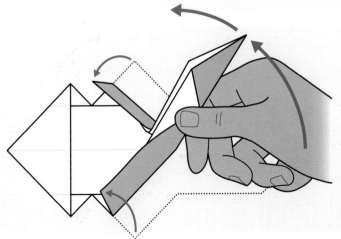

Lift up the right side, squeezing the fold together, and pushing it up upright, at the same time creasing the other two folds. Now push the piece in your right hand over and flatten down as shown in 16.

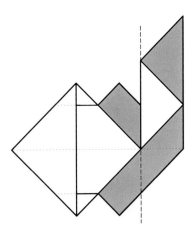

Note the position of the dashed line then go to step 17.

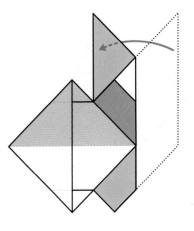

Fold the right part back and behind as shown. Crease.

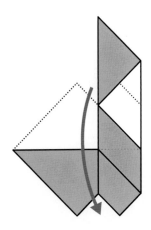

Now fold down the front top, shown as shaded in step 17, and crease.

Fold down the top point along the dashed line, crease and unfold.
Fold the other way on the same fold, crease and unfold.

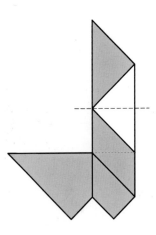

Repeat step 19 along the new dashed line shown.

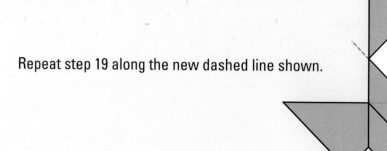

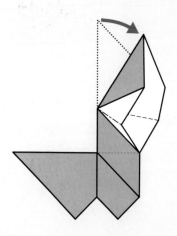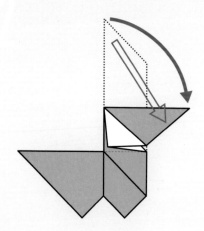

Holding the body in the right hand, take the top part in your left and push it down, making sure that the white areas on each side fold down over the red 'neck' part, as shown here in steps 21 and 22.

Make and crease the two folds on the tail and the three on the head.

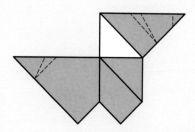

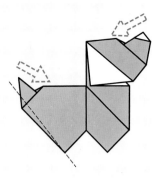

Open the head and fold back along the small fold to make the nose. Re-fold the head together and crimp fold on the other two creases.
Crimp fold the tail.

Fold in each side of the back leg and tail as indicated.

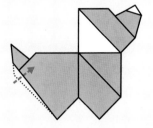

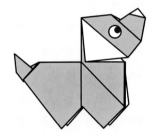

Add eyes and the little dog is finished.

Giraffe

This model contains a few more hard folds.

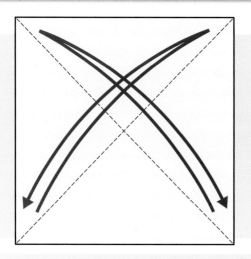

1 Start with a square, coloured side up. Fold the bottom left corner up to the top right, crease and unfold. Repeat with the bottom right corner up to the top left.

2 Fold the bottom edge up to the top one, crease and unfold. Repeat with the right edge over to the left one.

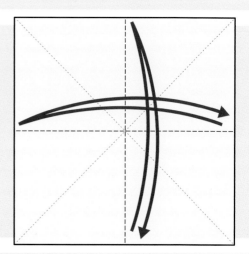

3

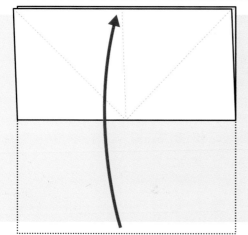

Fold the bottom edge up to the top one and crease.

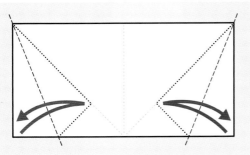

Fold the left edge to the diagonal crease.
Crease well and unfold. Unfold the sheet.

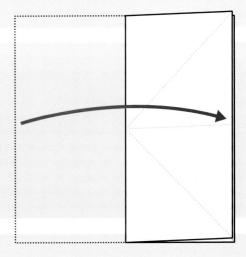

Now fold the left edge over to the
right one and crease.

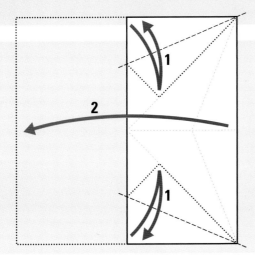

Fold the top and bottom edges into the
diagonal creases as in step 4 and
unfold the sheet again.

Turn the sheet white side up and
turn through 45°.

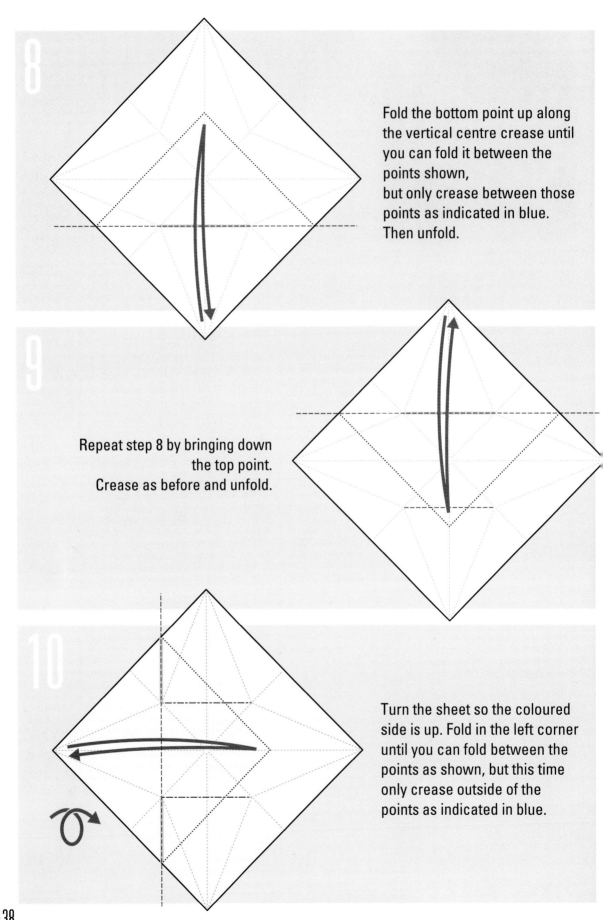

8

Fold the bottom point up along the vertical centre crease until you can fold it between the points shown,
but only crease between those points as indicated in blue.
Then unfold.

9

Repeat step 8 by bringing down the top point.
Crease as before and unfold.

10

Turn the sheet so the coloured side is up. Fold in the left corner until you can fold between the points as shown, but this time only crease outside of the points as indicated in blue.

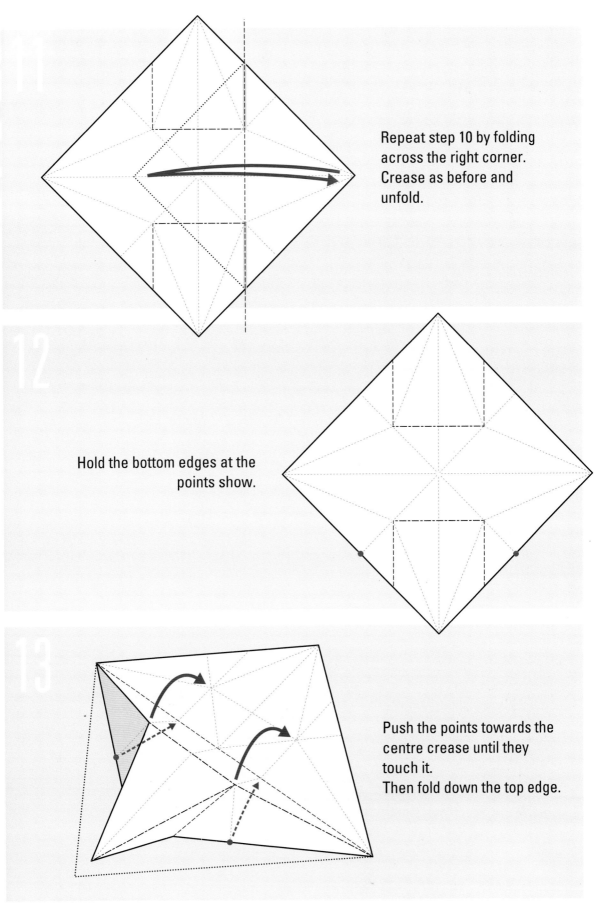

Repeat step 10 by folding across the right corner. Crease as before and unfold.

Hold the bottom edges at the points show.

Push the points towards the centre crease until they touch it.
Then fold down the top edge.

14 Fold down the front point, tucking in the two sides.

15 It should look like this now.

16 Turn over. Now fold this side the same as you did the other.

17 Now it looks like this.

18 Inside reverse fold the left point.

19 Fold the front and back points on the left of the model to the positions shown.

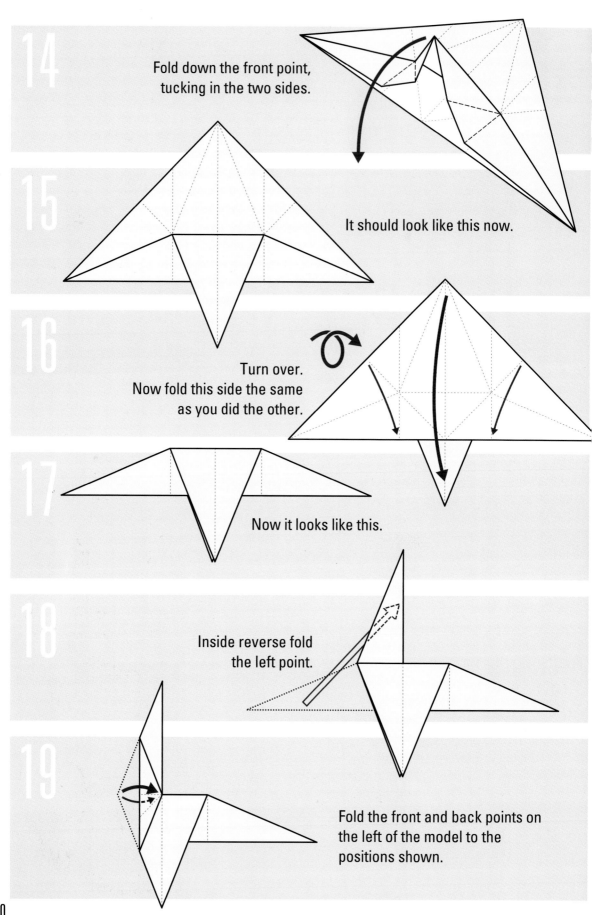

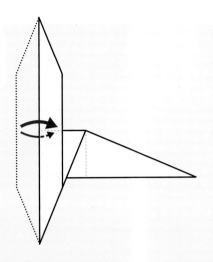

Fold the front and back edges on the left of the model to the positions shown.

Fold over the right point as shown, crease and unfold. Fold the other way on the same fold, crease and unfold.

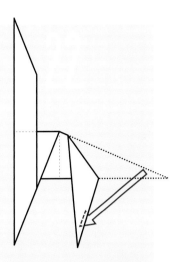

Outside reverse fold.

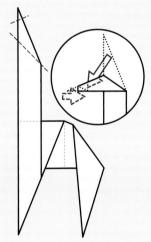

Fold and crease as shown and then outside reverse fold on the big one to create the head. Inside reverse the small fold to create the nose.

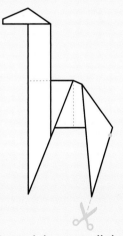

Cut as indicated, but not all the way to the top, to create two back legs.

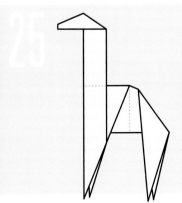

The finished model. Well done if yours looks like this!

Dove

The first two folds in the model of the 'Cicada' (page 30) are used to start to make this flying dove.

1

Start with a white square. Fold the bottom corner up to the top and crease.

2

Fold the left point over to the right one, crease and unfold.

3

Fold the left and right points up to the top corner and crease.

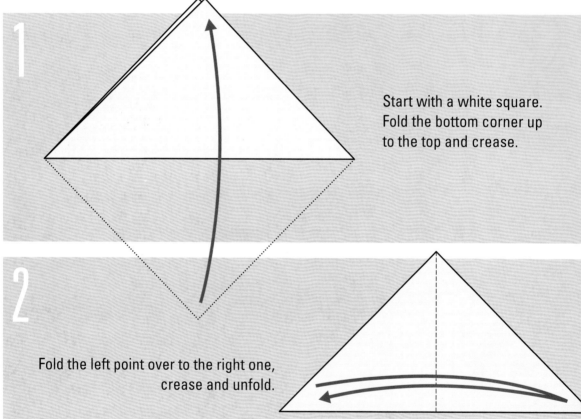

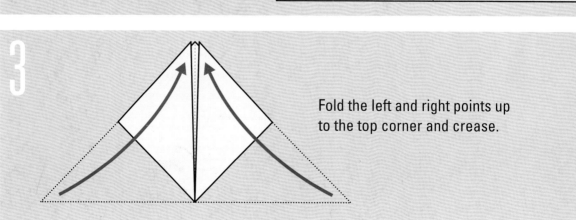

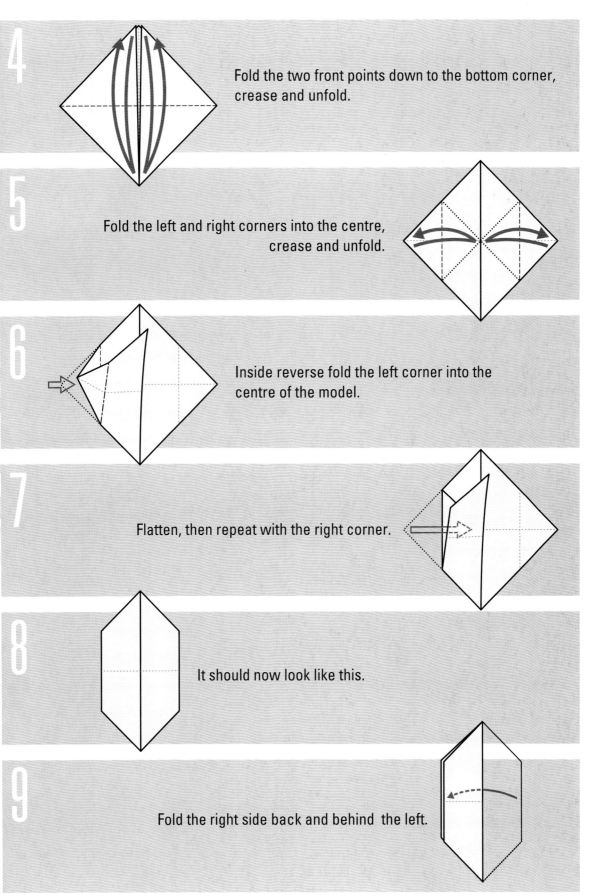

4 Fold the two front points down to the bottom corner, crease and unfold.

5 Fold the left and right corners into the centre, crease and unfold.

6 Inside reverse fold the left corner into the centre of the model.

7 Flatten, then repeat with the right corner.

8 It should now look like this.

9 Fold the right side back and behind the left.

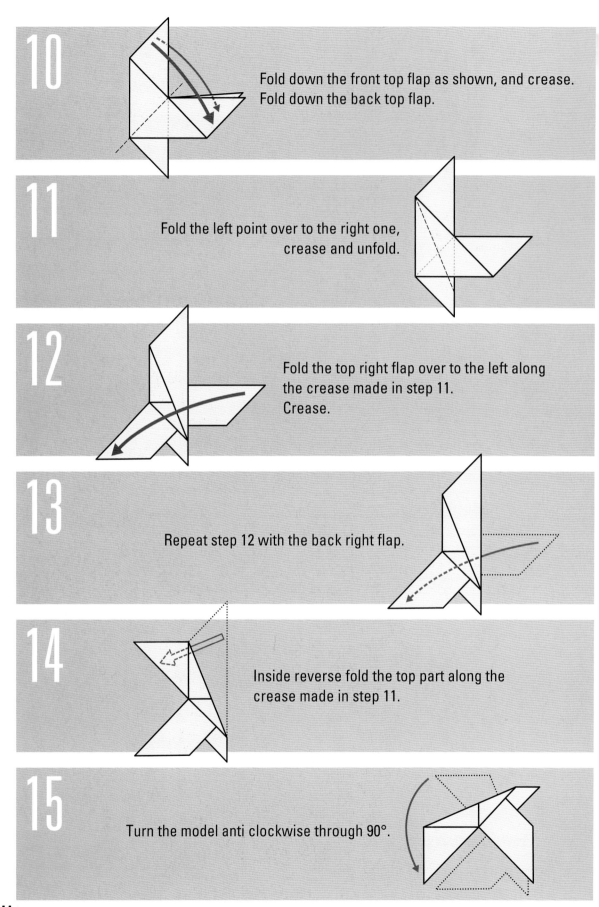

10 Fold down the front top flap as shown, and crease. Fold down the back top flap.

11 Fold the left point over to the right one, crease and unfold.

12 Fold the top right flap over to the left along the crease made in step 11. Crease.

13 Repeat step 12 with the back right flap.

14 Inside reverse fold the top part along the crease made in step 11.

15 Turn the model anti clockwise through 90°.

16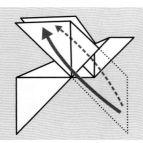

Fold up both wings as shown.

17

Fold and crease the tail and the head.
Unfold, and then fold and crease the other way.

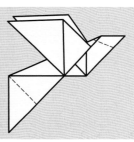

18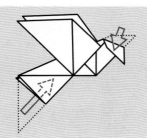

Inside reverse fold the tail.
Outside reverse fold the head.

19

Your dove is now finished.

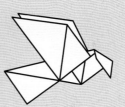

Camel

To start this camel follow the first 9 steps from the 'Lizard Head' (page 66) to make the preliminary base. Then follow the first 10 steps from the 'Crow' (page 72) instructions.

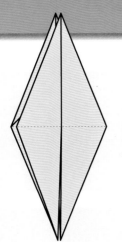

Start with the bird base as shown here.

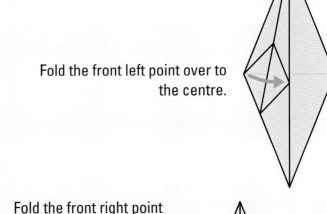

Fold the front left point over to the centre.

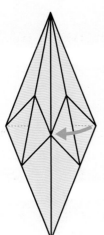

Fold the front right point over to the centre.

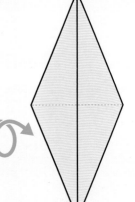

Turn the model over.

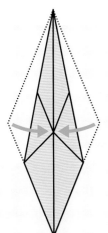

Repeat steps 2 and 3 on this side.

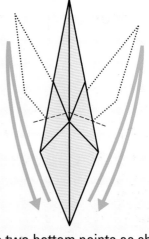

Fold up the two bottom points as shown (make the fold as high as possible without tearing the model). Crease, unfold, and then fold the other way on the same fold, crease and unfold.

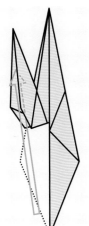

Inside reverse fold the left side and crease.

Inside reverse fold the right side and crease.

Model should look like ths now.

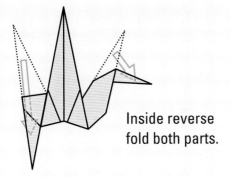

Inside reverse fold both parts.

Fold, crease and unfold along the two dashed lines. Fold the other way on the same folds, crease and unfold.

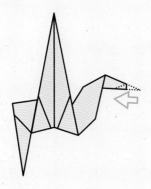

Inside reverse fold as shown.

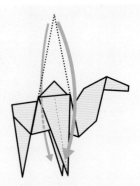

Fold down the two top points on each side to make front legs.

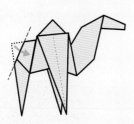

Fold inwards on each side on the dashed line indicated.

Open the rear flap and cut the middle of it as shown in blue to make two legs.

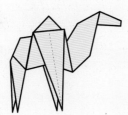

Your finished camel should look like this.

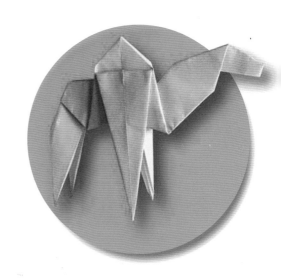

Elephant

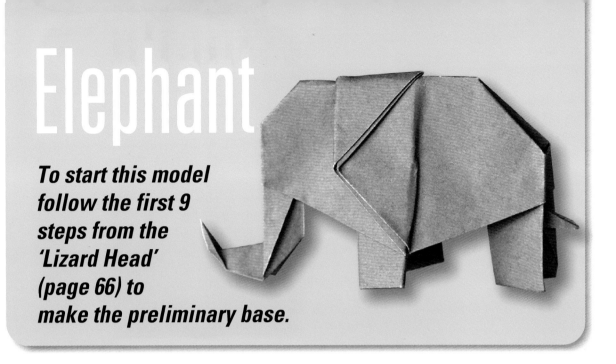

To start this model follow the first 9 steps from the 'Lizard Head' (page 66) to make the preliminary base.

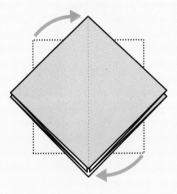

Turn through 45° so the four points are at the bottom.

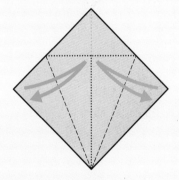

Fold the lower left edges into the centre and crease.
Repeat with lower right edges.

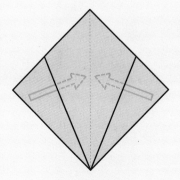

Inside reverse fold the two top flaps.

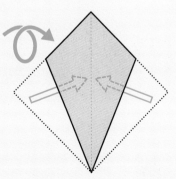

Turn over and inside reverse fold the remaining two flaps.

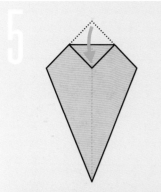

5 Fold down the top point and crease it when it is level with the two side points.

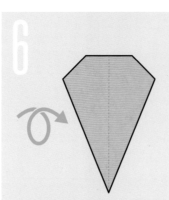

6 Turn the model over.

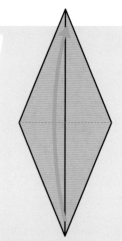

7 Take the front bottom point and fold it up and flatten.

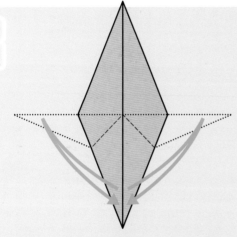

8 Fold up the two points to the positions shown and crease well, then unfold.

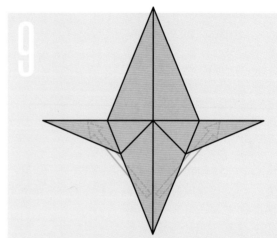

9 Inside reverse fold both parts.

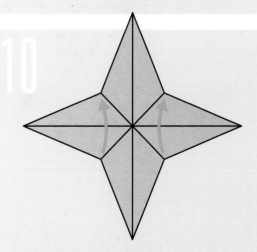

10 Fold up the front two middle flaps.

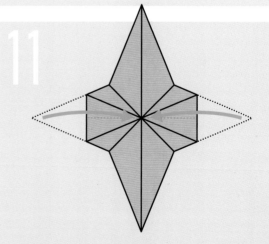

11 Fold the left and right points into the centre and crease well.

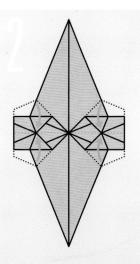

Fold the points of the small flaps into the centre and crease well.

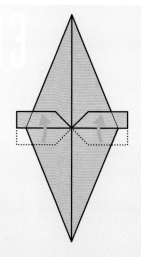

Fold up the bottom small flaps and crease well.

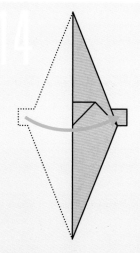

Fold in half by bringing the left side forward and over to the right.

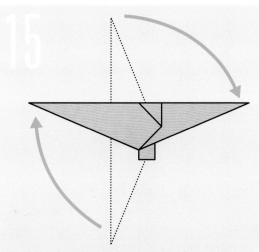

Turn the model through 90° clockwise.

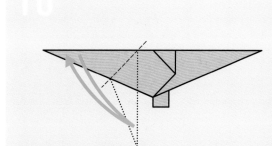

Fold, crease and unfold along the dashed line. Fold the other way on the same fold, crease and unfold.

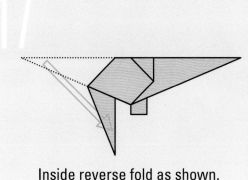

Inside reverse fold as shown.

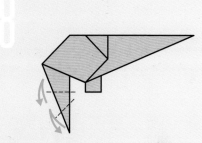

Fold and crease along the two dashed lines indicated.

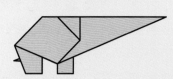 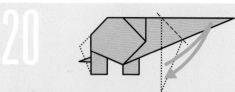

Inside reverse fold along the top fold to take the part inside. Then inside reverse fold the small bit to stick out for a tail.

Fold inside the the two flaps to shape the back of the elephant. Fold, crease and unfold along the dashed line. Fold the other way on the same fold, crease and unfold.

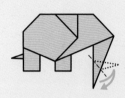 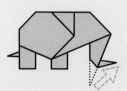

Inside reverse fold to make the trunk. Then fold, crease and unfold along the dashed line. Fold the other way on the same fold, crease and unfold.

Inside reverse fold.

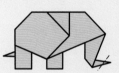 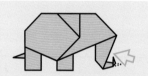

Inside reverse fold.

Fold and crease as indicated.

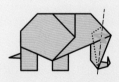 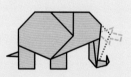

Outside reverse fold.

Fold, crease and unfold the two sides as indicated.

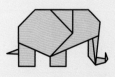

Inside reverse fold the two sides.

The finished model!

Crab

To start this model follow the first 9 steps from the 'Lizard Head' (page 66) to make the preliminary base.

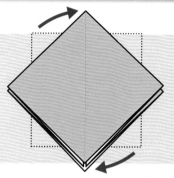

1 Turn through 45° so the four points are at the bottom.

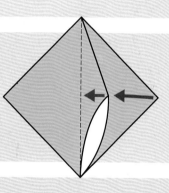

2 Lift up the right front corner and open up the flap with your finger.

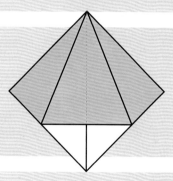

3 Press the centre fold down until it sits over the centre and then flatten.

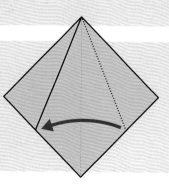

4 Fold the right side of the new flap over to the left and flatten.

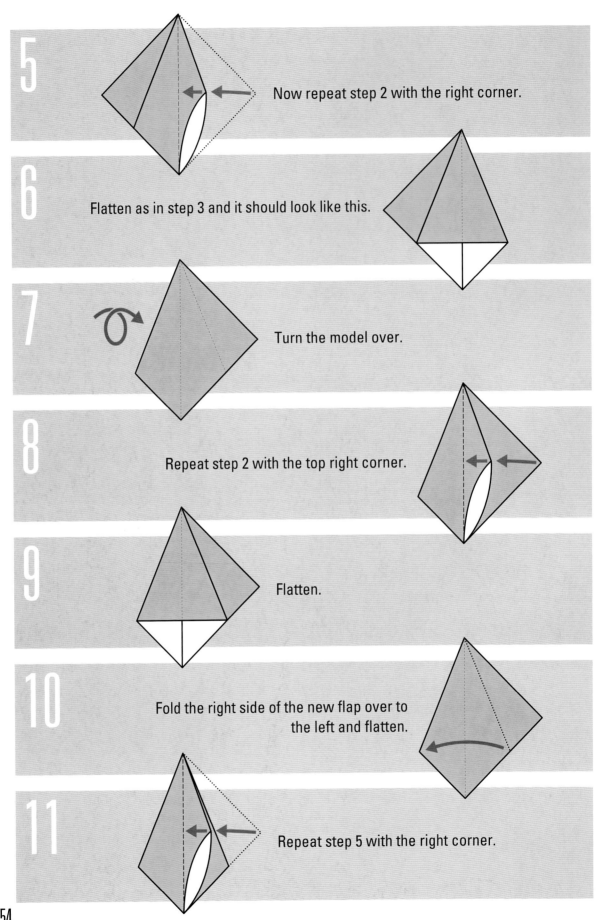

5 Now repeat step 2 with the right corner.

6 Flatten as in step 3 and it should look like this.

7 Turn the model over.

8 Repeat step 2 with the top right corner.

9 Flatten.

10 Fold the right side of the new flap over to the left and flatten.

11 Repeat step 5 with the right corner.

Flatten. Looking from the top you should have four flaps on each side.

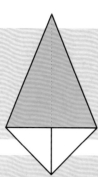

Fold the front left bottom edge into the centre, crease and unfold.
Repeat with the front right bottom edge.

Take the bottom centre of the front orange triangle and lift up and over.

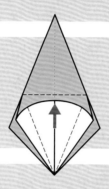

Keep pushing up and crease the two bottom edges and the fold that is now across the middle.

Flatten, and it should now look like this.

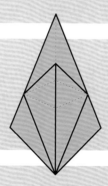

Fold the left and right edges of the new folds to the centre and crease.

Turn over.

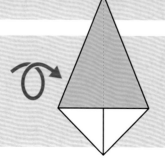

19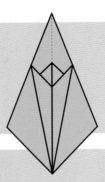

Repeat steps 13 to 17 with this side and it should then look like this.

20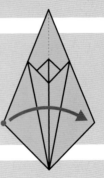

Take the front left point indicated and fold over to the right and crease.

21

It will now look like this.

22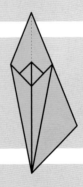

Repeat steps 13 to 17 with this side and it will look like this.

23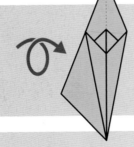

Turn over.

24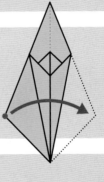

Take the front left point indicated and fold over to the right and crease.

25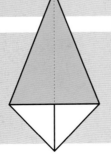

It will now look like this.

26

Repeat steps 13 to 17 with this side and it will look like this.

27

Fold the top back and down along the dashed line and tuck behind the tab that sticks up.

28

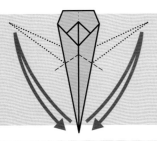

Fold up the legs as shown, crease and unfold. Fold the other way on the same fold, crease and unfold.

29

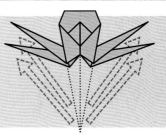

Inside reverse fold each of the legs and crease into the postions shown.

30

Inside reverse fold each of the legs at the positions shown.

31

Add eyes to complete the model.

Polar bear

Because of the number of folds in this model it gets quite 'thick' so it will need some careful creasing.

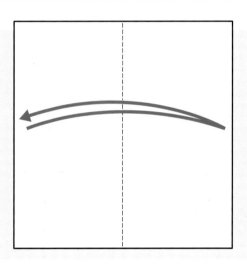

Start with a white square and fold the left edge over to the right, crease and unfold.

Fold the left and right edges into the centre and crease.

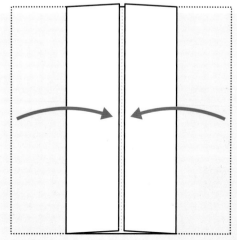

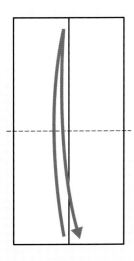

Fold the bottom edge up to the top, crease and unfold.

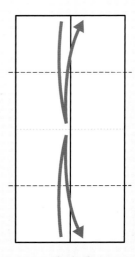

Fold the top and bottom edges into the centre, crease and unfold.

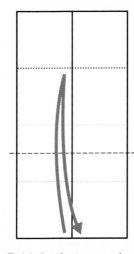

Fold the bottom edge up to the top crease created in step 4, crease and unfold.

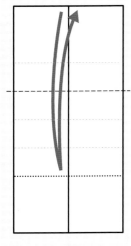

Fold the top edge down to the bottom crease created in step 4, crease and unfold.

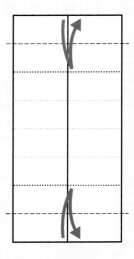

Fold the top edge down to the top crease created in step 4, crease and unfold. Fold the bottom edge up to the bottom crease created in step 4, crease and unfold.

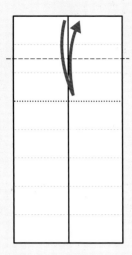

Fold the top edge down
to the 3rd crease.
Then crease and unfold.

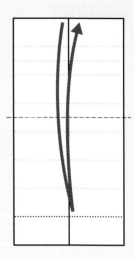

Fold down the top edge
to the bottom fold,
crease and unfold.

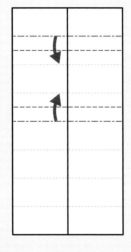

Recrease the two folds
indicated the other way
as mountain folds.

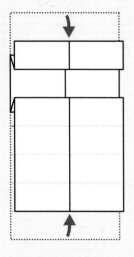

Fold to the shape as shown.

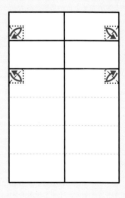

Fold and unfold the four
little corners.

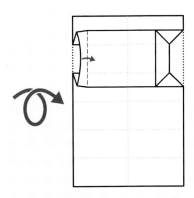

Turn the model over. Fold over and in the edges between the horizontal folds and flatten as shown.

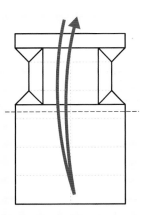

Fold down the top to create a new fold at the place shown. Crease and unfold.

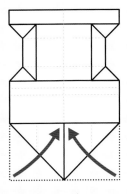

Fold up the two corners to the centre and crease.

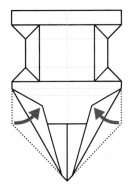

Fold in each side as shown. Crease well.

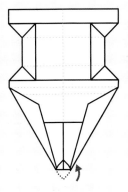

Fold up the tip.

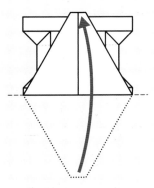

Fold up the bottom to the top along the fold created in step 14.

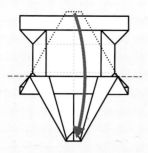

Fold down the top along the dashed line indicated.

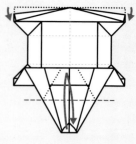

Fold down the top two corners as shown as crease. Fold up the bottom as shown, crease and unfold.

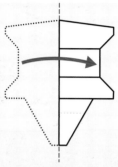

Fold the model in half by bringing the left half forward and over to the right.

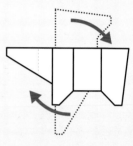

Turn the model clockwise through 90°.

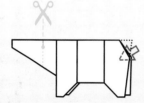

Cut down on the outer sides of the head a couple of millimetres and curl forward the front bits to create the ears. Inside reverse fold the back as shown to shape the back of the bear.

Add eyes and nose to finish the model.

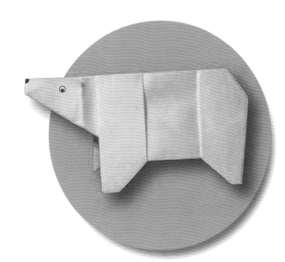

Dragonfly

To start this model follow the first 9 steps from the 'Lizard Head' (page 66) to make the preliminary base.
Then follow the first 10 steps from the 'Crow' (page 72) instructions.

1 Start with the bird base as shown here.

2 Fold the front top point down to the bottom.

3 Turn the model over.

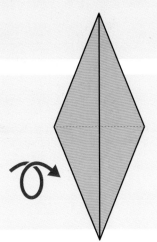

4

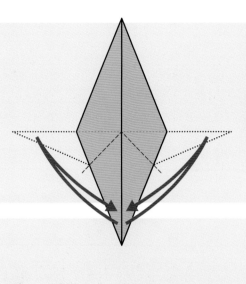

Fold up the front two bottom points, crease and unfold.

5

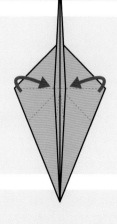

Take the two front sides and lift them up.

6

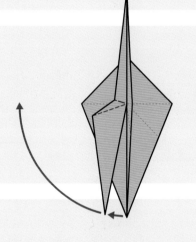

Hold the bottom of the left side and push up and to the left.

7

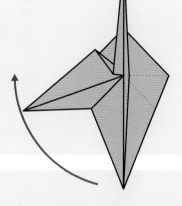

Fold up as here.

8

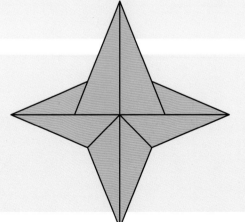

Do the same with the right side and your model should look like this.

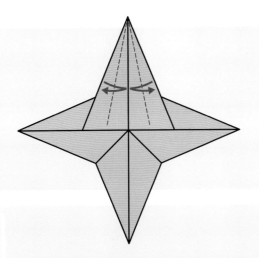

Fold the outside edges of the top part into the centre, crease and unfold.

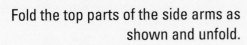

Fold the top parts of the side arms as shown and unfold.

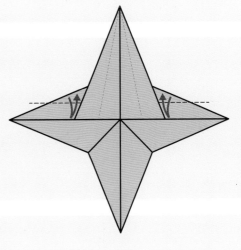

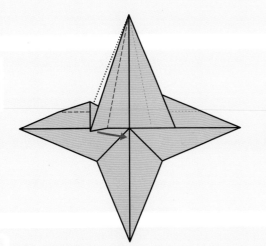

Fold the point across to the centre as shown, folding down the top of the side arm.

Flatten the area to look like this. Repeat with the right side

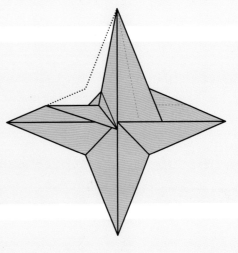

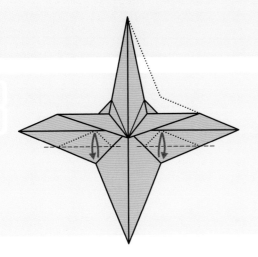

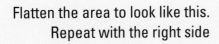

Fold the bottom points of the lower side arms up to the centre, crease and unfold.

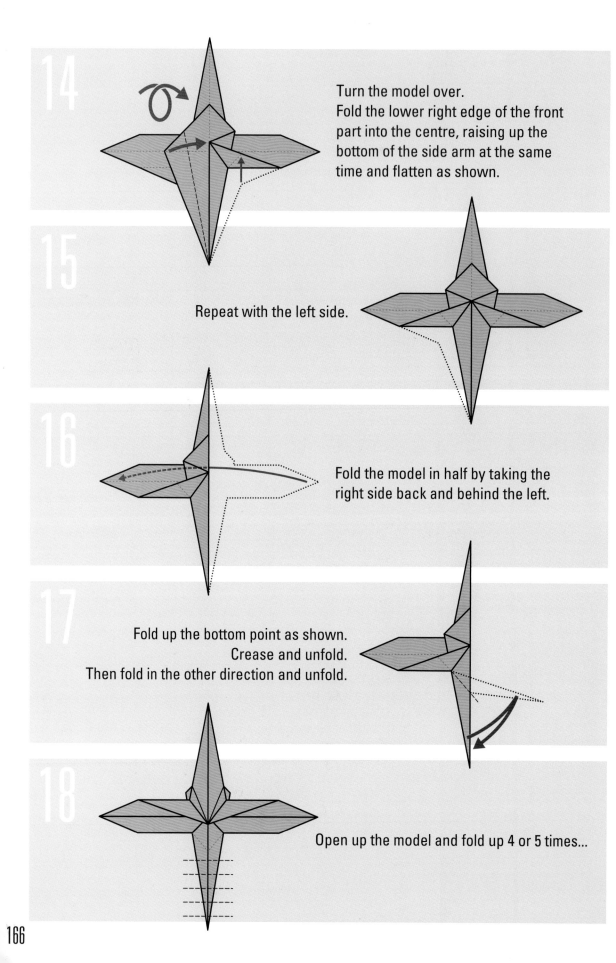

14

Turn the model over.
Fold the lower right edge of the front part into the centre, raising up the bottom of the side arm at the same time and flatten as shown.

15

Repeat with the left side.

16

Fold the model in half by taking the right side back and behind the left.

17

Fold up the bottom point as shown.
Crease and unfold.
Then fold in the other direction and unfold.

18

Open up the model and fold up 4 or 5 times...

19

...to create the head.

20

Fold the wings down at the places shown and crease. Cut through the wings to make two each side.

21

Shape your model as here. It should now look like this.

Inflatable frog

To start this model follow the first 9 steps from the 'Lizard Head' (page 66) to make the preliminary base.

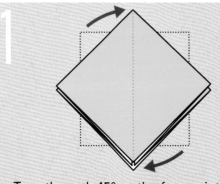

1 Turn through 45° so the four points are at the bottom.

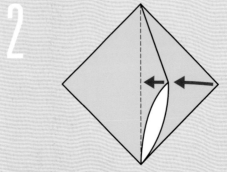

2 Lift up the right front corner and open up the flap with your finger.

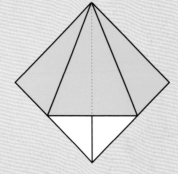

3 Press the centre fold down until it sits over the centre and then flatten.

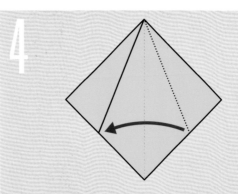

4 Fold the right side of the new flap over to the left and flatten.

5 Now repeat step 2 with the right corner.

6 Flatten as in step 3 and it should look like this.

7 Turn the model over.

8 Repeat step 2 with the top right corner.

9 Flatten.

10 Fold the right side of the new flap over to the left and flatten.

11 Repeat step 5 with the right corner.

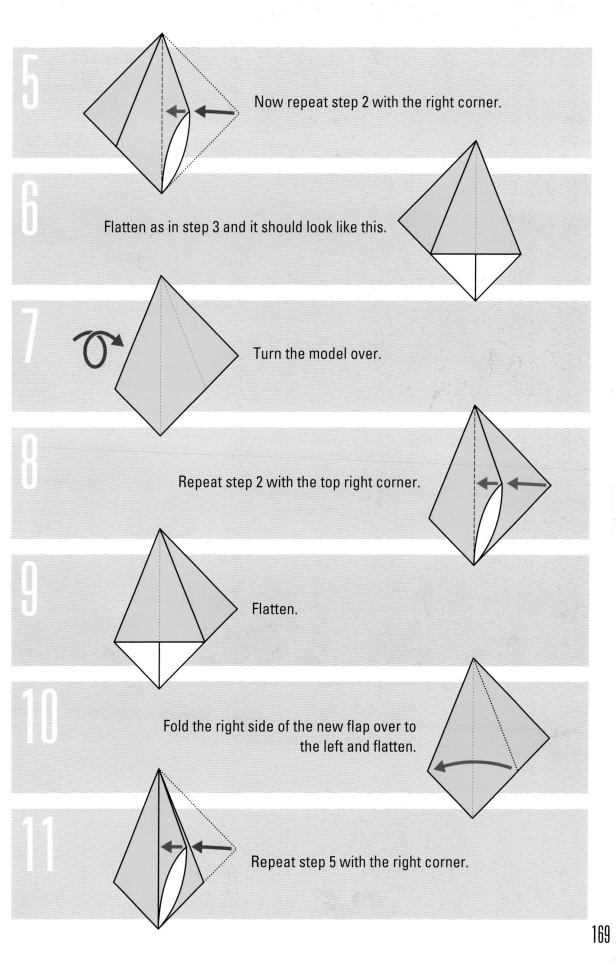

12

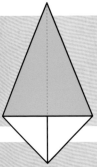

Flatten.
Looking from the top you should have four flaps on each side.

13

Fold the front left bottom edge into the centre, crease and unfold.
Repeat with the front right bottom edge.

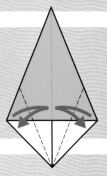

14

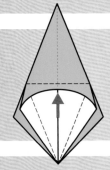

Take the bottom centre of the front green triangle and lift up and over.

15

Keep pushing up and crease the two bottom edges and the fold that is now across the middle.

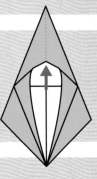

16

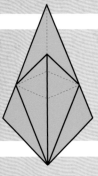

Flatten, and it should now look like this.

17

Turn over.

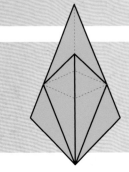

18

Repeat steps 13 to 16 with this side and it should then look like this.

19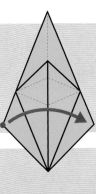

Take the front left point indicated and fold over to the right and crease.

20

It will now look like this.

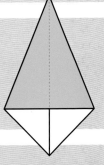

21

Fold the front left bottom edge into the centre, crease and unfold.
Repeat with the front right bottom edge.

22

Take the bottom centre of the front green triangle and lift up and over.

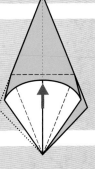

23

Keep pushing up and crease the two bottom edges and the fold that is now across the middle.

24

Flatten, and it should now look like this.

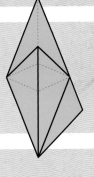

25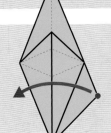

Take the front right point indicated and fold over to the left and crease.

26 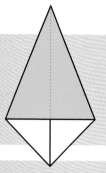 It will now look like this.

27 Repeat steps 13 to 16 with this side and it should then look like this.

28  Fold the front right side point over to the left to expose a blank face. Turn the back faces over to expose the same blank face as the front. Keep turning until you have four points on each side when viewed from the top.

29 It should now look like this.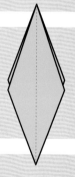

30 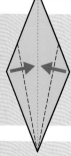 Fold the lower edges of the front flaps along the dashed lines.

31 Crease and it should look like this.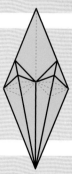

32 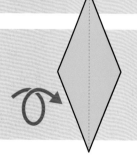 Turn over.

33 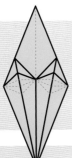 Repeat steps 30 and 31 and it should look like this.

34 Fold the left side point over to the right to expose a blank face. Repeat with the back to reveal the other blank side.

35 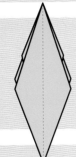 It should look like this now.

36 Repeat steps 30 to 33 on both sides and it will look like this.

37  Turn the front left over to the right and then the back right to the left so that it looks like this.

38 Fold up the two front points as shown, crease and unfold.

39 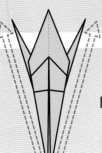 Inside reverse fold to create the front legs.

40

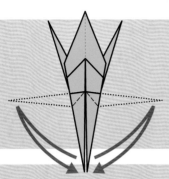

Fold up the two front points as shown, crease and unfold.

41

Inside reverse fold to create the back legs.

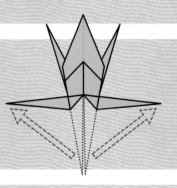

42

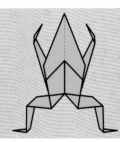

Shape the back and front legs as shown using inside reverse folds.

43

Hold the back legs and blow sharply into the body where indicated to inflate the frog.

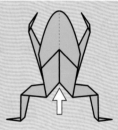

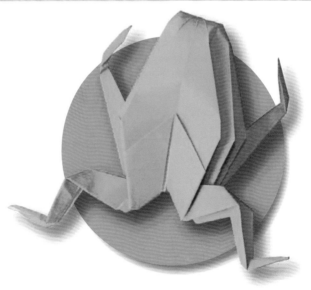